modern baby
CROCHET

PATTERNS FOR DECORATING, PLAYING, AND SNUGGLING

Stacey Trock

Martingale
Create with Confidence

Modern Baby Crochet:
Patterns for Decorating, Playing, and Snuggling
© 2014 by Stacey Trock

Martingale®
19021 120th Ave. NE, Ste. 102
Bothell, WA 98011-9511 USA
ShopMartingale.com

Printed in China
19 18 17 16 15 14   8 7 6 5 4 3 2 1

Library of Congress Cataloging-in-Publication Data
is available upon request.

ISBN: 978-1-60468-339-4

Mission Statement
Dedicated to providing quality products and service to inspire creativity.

CREDITS

PRESIDENT AND CEO: Tom Wierzbicki

EDITOR IN CHIEF: Mary V. Green

DESIGN DIRECTOR: Paula Schlosser

MANAGING EDITOR: Karen Costello Soltys

ACQUISITIONS EDITOR: Karen M. Burns

TECHNICAL EDITOR: Susan Huxley

COPY EDITOR: Marcy Heffernan

PRODUCTION MANAGER: Regina Girard

COVER AND INTERIOR DESIGNER: Adrienne Smitke

PHOTOGRAPHER: Brent Kane

ILLUSTRATORS: Cheryl Fall and Kathryn Silva Conway

Contents

Introduction

I've always loved crocheting for babies . . . the projects are small and irresistibly cute! When I wrote my first book, *Cuddly Crochet* (Martingale, 2010), which featured stuffed animals, blankets, and hats for babies, I discovered that oodles of you love crocheting animals and items for tiny ones as well! So, I think now's a great time for another crochet baby book. I hope you love it!

In this book, I focused on the hub of baby life: the nursery. I wanted to create a book of baby designs that would suit any modern nursery, whimsical and adorable, but with a chic twist. And whether you're looking to decorate an entire room, make a few accent pieces, or simply whip up a project to give as a gift, I think you'll find exactly what you're looking for in these pages.

Modern babies aren't stuck in a pastel world. Their nurseries can be decorated in rainbow colors, neutrals, or even black and white. The only rule that guides modern baby decor is that it has to be adorable! I've designed 21 baby-friendly patterns: beautiful blankets, entrancing mobiles, whimsical plush toys, and even an ottoman and a rug, and showcased them in three fabulous color stories. I can't get enough of the lime-turquoise-orange combo in the Funky Argyle Pillow and Afghan (the projects aren't as hard as they look; see pages 27 and 31), and I've already claimed the lovely gray Asymmetrical Basket-Weave Blanket (page 71) for myself. (Hey, nothing wrong with that!)

It's always my goal as a crochet designer and instructor to empower crocheters. Not only do I hope you love my written patterns, I also hope you make use of the tips included in this book to improve your crochet skills and to make the designs your own. Go ahead, try that new stitch. Switch up the color palette in that afghan. You can do it! Together, we can fill the world with precious handmade creations.

Stacey

Getting Started

Choosing the right yarn and notions and getting some crochet basics under your belt are the keys to a successful project. In this section, I'll tell you everything you need to know to get your project on the right track. Feel free to flip back to these pages for reference as you crochet.

CHOOSING YARNS

There are a dazzling variety of yarns available in today's market, and I've made sure to crochet each sample in this book using yarns, that are appropriate for a sweet little baby. Even though I've picked some pretty great yarns, you shouldn't feel tied to my choices. Part of the fun of making an item yourself is that you have complete control over the creative process, meaning you can experiment with yarns and colors to your heart's content.

While I want you to feel free to substitute yarns, you can't just swap them willy-nilly. Yarns come in different thicknesses, and selecting a yarn that's thicker or thinner than the one specified for your project will result in a smaller or larger piece than mine.

I suggest substituting a yarn that's the same thickness and fiber as the yarn used to crochet the projects shown in this book. For example, if the yarn used in the project is a worsted-weight wool yarn, then selecting another wool yarn with the same icon on its label (⬛) will be a good fit. (Have a peek at the "Standard Yarn Weights" chart on page 78 for more information.)

And, of course, don't forget about crocheting a gauge swatch . . . that's the way you'll check that you're using the right yarn/hook size for your project. A gauge swatch isn't scary; I'll walk you through making one on page 6!

Machine-Washable Yarns

Let's be honest: babies are messy little people.

What's the nicest thing you can do for a new mom, besides crocheting a lovely gift for baby? Make sure that the item is also easy to care for. I recommend selecting a yarn that's machine washable. When you're shopping for yarn, read the care instructions on the yarn label—all the information you need is there.

If you're crocheting a project that isn't intended to be played with by little ones, such as a mobile or bookends, then you have more flexibility in selecting your yarn. It won't be washed often, so choosing a machine-washable yarn isn't crucial.

Color Palette

While pastels are timeless, modern babies have lots of color options. You can select shockingly bright colors, a rainbow palette, primary colors, or even neutrals. I've crocheted the projects using some color combinations that I think are fun and appealing.

If your baby's nursery has a pink-and-white theme, should you pass up the gray Asymmetrical Basket-Weave Blanket (see page 71)? Of course not! Crochet it in pink! Make the colors work for the nursery that you have. I hope you're inspired by the colors I've chosen, but feel empowered to use colors that will turn the projects in this book into the perfect items for you!

Are You Giving a Gift?

When I'm giving a crocheted item as a gift, I enclose a label from the yarn I used for the project in the bundle. This way, the recipient has the washing instructions on hand.

GAUGE

We can't talk about crocheting without a little chat about gauge. Each project in this book has a specified gauge, that is, the number of stitches per inch using the specified yarn and the specified hook.

To check your gauge, crochet a square (if working in rows) or a circle (if working in rounds) that's the size indicated in the pattern instructions (usually about 4"). Then count the number of stitches you have to see if they're close to the gauge given for the pattern.

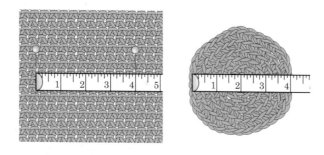

Everyone crochets differently, so a swatch using your own crocheting style will tell you if you're using the correct size hook. If you have too many stitches and rows or rounds in your swatch, try a larger hook size. If you have too few, then try a smaller hook size. Keep making swatches (using different hook sizes) until you get one with the right number of stitches.

Right about now, most people wonder if they *really* have to do a gauge swatch. And the answer is, *"It depends."*

If you want your crocheted piece to be the same size as mine (which might be important, for example, if you're crocheting a pillow cover that needs to fit a specific-sized pillow form), then the answer is, *"Yes, you do need to crochet a gauge swatch."*

If you're crocheting a piece where size isn't terribly important (so what if your blanket is 1" bigger than mine?), then a gauge swatch is something you can skip. It's still nice to make one to see if you like the way the crocheted fabric is turning out.

CROCHET HOOKS

When you walk into a yarn shop or craft store, you'll notice a dazzling variety of hooks. Not only do crochet hooks come in different sizes, but they're made in a range of different materials and can flaunt a variety of features, such as a thumb rest or an ergonomic handle.

The most important thing is to choose the crochet hook that works for you. If you pick up a hook and it doesn't sit well in your hand or seems to make crocheting difficult, then give it a pass. Some people experience trouble learning to crochet only to find out that it's the hook that's the problem! You may have to try a few different ones to find your favorite, but the search for a hook that gives you a pleasant crocheting experience is worth it!

Hooks come in a variety of sizes, and the size is usually written on the hook. Select the size that's called for in the pattern.

But keep in mind that once you crochet your gauge swatch, you may find that you need a smaller or larger hook than is recommended. That's OK! Use the size hook that gives you the gauge you need for the project.

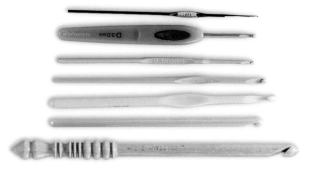

A variety of crochet hooks

Holding the Hook

If you're having difficulty crocheting, the problem may be with how you're holding your hook. When you wrap the yarn over your hook, the front of the hook should be facing you. When it's time to pull the yarn through the loop on the hook, rotate your hook downward. This way, the hook slides easily through the loop, instead of getting caught on it.

OTHER SUPPLIES

While your yarn and hook are certainly essential to your crochet project, there are a few other items you'll need to complete the projects in this book. Most of these items can be found at your local craft store. For unique items that aren't regularly stocked, check "Resources" on page 79 for contact information.

Stuffing and Pillow Forms

I designed a few stuffed animal projects for this book, and they require, well, stuffing. I use polyester fiberfill, which is inexpensive, hypoallergenic, and readily available by the bag in your local craft store.

Different brands have different amounts of fluffiness, so it's always best to go with what feels best to you! In addition to polyester, there are a number of different stuffing fibers available, including cotton and bamboo. While many fibers work, I don't recommend using wool as stuffing for children's toys, as it isn't always machine washable and can be slow to dry. If your little one has a good slobber on a toy, you don't want the insides to stay damp. Eeew.

A pillow form (or insert) is stuffing that's enclosed in a sewn casing or preformed into a pillow shape. A variety of sizes and shapes of pillow forms are available at your craft store, and they're an incredibly handy format for getting the exact amount of stuffing in the shape you need.

Felt

You've probably seen paper-sized sheets of felt in your local craft store. This type of felt is great for adding fun details to your crocheted pieces. Don't feel like embroidering the tooth on Zabby the Giggle Monster (page 23)? Cut a triangle out of white felt and sew it on!

Felt is also available by the yard, just like fabric, and it's this type that I use as a stabilizer and backing for the rug (page 67) and playmat (page 49) in this book. It's about ⅛" thicker than the felt that comes in smaller sheets and is 36" wide, the perfect width for the projects in this book.

If you're lucky enough to find a great supplier for ¼" felt, then you're in good hands. In my experience, this thickness change causes the price to jump by a lot. No worries. To obtain the ¼" thickness called for in the projects in this book, purchase the craft-store felt and double it! You can easily sew through both layers as you stitch your rug or mat together.

Of course, you can use the mats in this book without felt, but the shape may become distorted and the fabric will wear more quickly than it would with a backing.

Locking Stitch Markers

Stitch markers are very handy for keeping track of your place when you're crocheting, particularly for marking the end of a round (see page 14). I recommend the locking varieties; they stay in place and won't fall off.

Another handy use for locking stitch markers is to pin together two pieces that you're attaching. This will ensure that your pieces are properly aligned (and remain so!) while you're doing your attaching.

Locking stitch marker

Tapestry Needles

Tapestry needles are used for sewing pieces together or for weaving in ends (see page 15). They're very similar to sewing needles, but they have a blunt tip and a larger eye, suitable for yarn.

Tapestry needles come in metal or plastic and in a variety of sizes. The material you choose is a matter of personal preference: plastic needles are cheaper, but also prone to breakage. As for size, as long as your yarn fits through the eye of the needle, you're set!

Top: *plastic straight needle;*
bottom: *metal needle with bent tip*

Crocheter's Toolbox

There are a few notions that you'll find yourself reaching for over and over again. I bundle up these essentials into a little toolbox and carry it around with me all the time. This way, I always have what I need.

My essentials include: a tapestry needle, a retractable measuring tape, a dozen locking stitch markers, and scissors. If you have a big toolbox, you can toss your favorite hook sizes in as well. For the projects in this book, assume you'll need your toolbox, as I haven't mentioned these items individually in the "Hooks and Notions" list for each project.

Rattles and Squeakers and Crinkle—Oh My!

A number of projects call for rattle inserts or crinkle paper. These delightful additions make your project extra fun and interactive for little ones. Once you start using them, you may find yourself looking for excuses to sneak them into other projects! If you can't find these in your store, check "Resources" (page 79).

Animal Eyes

This book contains stuffed animals that feature animal eyes, which, excitingly, come in a wide range of colors. These safety eyes are made with a post on the back and are fastened with a metal or plastic washer. They're beautiful (and add a professional look), but aren't recommended for children under three years of age.

Baby-Safe Crocheted Eyes

If you're making stuffed animals, especially the Sweet Tweeter! (page 75), for a little one under three years old, it's safest to crochet or embroider the eyes. Here's a pattern to crochet the eyes:

With black yarn, ch 2.

Sc 6 times in 2nd ch from hook. 6 sts

Fasten off with long tail and use a running stitch (page 15) to attach to head. Repeat for second eye.

Anatomy of a Stitch

If you're familiar with crocheting, you may not think of a stitch as having parts, but it does. In this book, we'll do some fun textured stitches that make use of different parts of the stitch. Let's learn about these parts first, shall we?

FRONT AND BACK LOOPS

When you make a crochet stitch, you end up with two loops at the top of the stitch: a front loop and a back loop. In the patterns in this book, you will use the front, back, or both loops!

Through the front loop (fl): You will occasionally be instructed to crochet through the front loop of a stitch, usually to create a textured effect such as the bobble stitch (see page 13), or to add an edging, as in Pastel Petals Afghan on page 43.

Through the back loop (bl): Some patterns in this book instruct you to crochet through the back loop only. This leaves a little ridge (the unused front loop) that I think is cute and helps with attaching the pieces.

Through both loops: Crocheting through both loops is standard crochet protocol. It's the default technique used, and it creates a denser fabric than either of the two previous stitches.

Left: *stitches through back loop only;*
right: *stitches through both loops*

WORKING AROUND THE POST

The vertical portion of the stitch, below the loops, is the *post*.

While we usually think of crocheting as working through the loops, as described at left, you can also work around the post for a textured effect. This portion is barely visible in single crochet, but is pronounced in taller stitches such as double crochet.

There are two stitches that use the post: front-post double crochet (fpdc) and back-post double crochet (bpdc). Details on each of these fun stitches are on page 12.

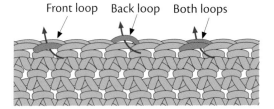

Front loop   Back loop   Both loops

Crochet Stitches

Below you'll find an explanation of the stitches used in this book. Notice that some stitches have an abbreviation that is used in the instructions to save space. A complete list of abbreviations used in this book is on page 79.

SLIPKNOT

The slipknot is how crochet stitches are born. Every piece begins with a slipknot, even though it's not explicitly mentioned in the pattern. To work, make a loop about 3" from the end of the yarn. Now pull the working yarn through the loop and put the resulting loop on your hook. Pull the yarn to tighten, and you're ready to start crocheting!

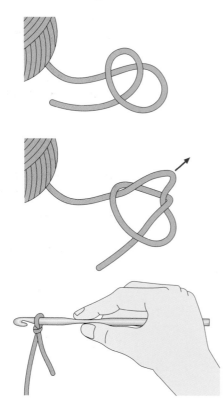

CHAIN (ch)

Each pattern specifies the number of chain stitches needed to start, called the foundation chain. Begin with a slipknot. To make one chain stitch, wrap the yarn over your hook. Using your hook, pull the yarn through the loop on the hook. This action pulls the new loop onto the hook and makes one chain stitch. Repeat for the required number of chain stitches.

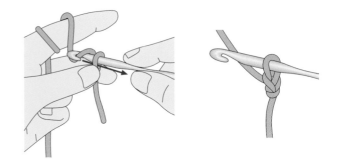

Chains: Not Just for Starting!

Chain stitches (usually between one and three) can also be made at the beginning of a row, where they collectively are called a *turning chain (tch)*. To work this, wrap the yarn over your hook and pull through the loop on your hook for each chain stitch, exactly the same way you make a foundation chain (see above).

SLIP STITCH (sl st)

To work a slip stitch, insert your hook into the next stitch and wrap the yarn over the hook. Pull the yarn through both loops on the hook.

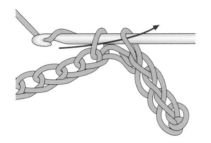

SINGLE CROCHET (sc)

Single crochet creates a dense fabric that is particularly useful for stuffed animals because it keeps the stuffing from poking through. To work, insert your hook into the specified stitch and wrap the yarn over the hook. Pull the yarn through the stitch.

There are now two loops on the hook. Wrap the yarn over your hook again and pull through both loops on the hook.

SINGLE CROCHET DECREASE (sc2tog, sc3tog)

To work a decrease in single crochet, insert your hook into the next stitch, wrap the yarn over the hook, and pull it through the stitch. Insert your hook into the next stitch, wrap the yarn over the hook, and pull it through the stitch—that's not a typo, do it twice! There are now three loops on your hook. Wrap the yarn over your hook again and pull it through all three loops on the hook. You now have one stitch where there used to be two.

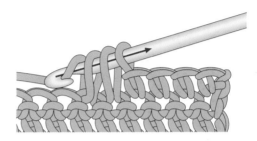

To decrease across larger numbers of stitches (such as sc3tog), you work the following as many times as the number of stitches you would like to decrease: insert your hook into the next stitch, wrap the yarn over the hook, and pull through the stitch. To finish, wrap the yarn over your hook and pull it through all remaining loops.

DOUBLE CROCHET (dc)

A double crochet is taller than a single crochet, and creates a softer, less dense fabric. It is also the foundation stitch for textured stitches such as front- and back-post double crochet. To work, wrap the yarn over your hook, then insert the hook into the indicated stitch.

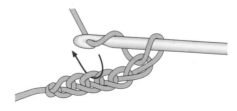

Wrap the yarn over your hook and pull through the stitch, giving you three loops on the hook. Wrap the yarn over your hook and pull through the first two loops on the hook.

Wrap the yarn over your hook again and pull through the two remaining loops on the hook.

DOUBLE CROCHET DECREASE (dc2tog, dc3tog)

Decreasing in double crochet is very similar to decreasing in single crochet (see page 11). Have a peek at the instructions for the single crochet decrease for details, and notice that the key to decreasing is working partial stitches.

To work a double crochet two together, begin with a double crochet stitch into the specified spot as you usually do, but do not pull the final loop through. Do the same partial double crochet stitch into the following and for as many stitches as you want to decrease across. You might end up with a lot of loops on your hook. That's OK!

To finish, wrap the yarn over your hook and pull through all remaining loops.

FRONT-POST DOUBLE CROCHET (fpdc)

The front-post double crochet is an interesting stitch that, over rows, creates the illusion of vertical lines across the piece.

To work, wrap the yarn over your hook as you would for basic double crochet. Insert your hook *from the front to the back, around the post* of the next stitch in the row below, and then *to the front*. Wrap the yarn over your hook and pull the loop to the front, giving you three loops on the hook. Wrap the yarn over your hook and pull through the first two loops on the hook. Wrap the yarn over your hook again and pull through the two remaining loops on the hook. Notice that the wrong side of a front-post double crochet looks like a back-post double crochet.

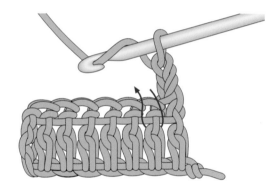

BACK-POST DOUBLE CROCHET (bpdc)

The back-post double crochet stitch creates the illusion of horizontal lines across the piece.

To work, wrap the yarn over the hook as you would for a basic double crochet. Insert your hook *from the back to the front, around the post* of the next stitch in the row below and then *to the back*. Wrap the yarn over your hook and pull the loop to the front and then to the back, giving you three loops on the hook. Wrap the yarn over your hook and pull through the first two loops. Wrap the yarn over your hook and pull through the two remaining loops on the hook. Notice that the wrong side of a back-post double crochet looks like a front-post double crochet.

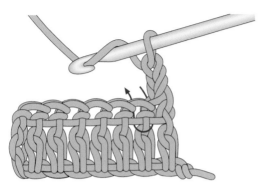

BOBBLE (bbl)

The bobble stitch is a fun, textured stitch that can be used on a single crochet fabric. Because you work in the round below your current round, you get a puff without the hole that other bobble stitches can leave behind. Working your single crochet stitches through the front loop only is crucial to achieve this stitch.

To work a bobble stitch, wrap the yarn over your hook, and then insert the hook into the front loop of the stitch *one row below* the next stitch. I like to insert the hook from the bottom to the top of the front loop, but you can work in the other direction too. In the current row, don't work the next stitch (the one behind the bobble); think of the bobble as taking this stitch's place.

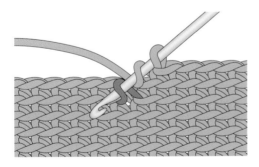

Wrap the yarn over your hook and pull through the stitch. This gives you three loops on the hook. Wrap the yarn over your hook and pull through the first two loops on your hook. Repeat from the start twice more (inserting your hook into the same stitch), until you have four loops on the hook.

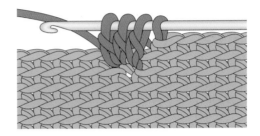

Wrap the yarn over your hook and pull through all the loops on your hook.

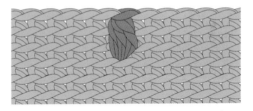

Additional Techniques

The following techniques will help you crochet the projects in this book and finish them with ease.

CHANGING COLORS

When you switch from one color to another, there is a trick to doing it so the change in color is very clean.

When a color change occurs in the middle of a row or round, work to one stitch before a color change (the illustration below shows the change in single crochet worked in a back loop, but the process is the same worked through both loops and for any other type of stitch). In the next stitch (the last one of your current color), crochet as usual, but do not wrap the yarn around the hook for the final loop. Instead, wrap the new color of yarn around your hook and pull the yarn through the remaining loop(s). Continue crocheting with the new color.

When a color change happens at the beginning of a row, changing colors means that you will need to introduce the new color (in the final "wrap and pull through") on the last stitch of the previous row.

FASTENING OFF

When you're finished crocheting, cut the yarn a couple of inches from your last stitch. Wrap the yarn over your hook and pull it through the last loop until the yarn end is all the way through. Tug—and you have a finished knot!

If the instructions say to "fasten off with long tail," leave about 12" of yarn before cutting the yarn and pulling it through the last loop. The long tail will be used for attaching your piece to another later on.

WORKING IN THE ROUND

Particularly when you're new to crochet, working in the round can be confusing. There is no clear indication where the round begins and ends, so it's easy to get lost. I recommend that you place a stitch marker in the last stitch at the end of the round. Then, after you've crocheted the stitches for the next round, you should end up exactly above the stitch marker. Move your stitch marker to the end of each round to keep track of where you are.

Follow the instructions and continue working in the round, without turning (unless told to do so in the pattern), until the piece is complete.

SURFACE CROCHET

This is a technique for adding a line of embellishment to a completed piece. Select where you'd like your design to begin. You can work in straight lines or in diagonal lines, as shown in the Funky Argyle projects on pages 27 and 31. With the right side of the work up, hold your yarn under your work and insert your hook from top to bottom at your starting point. Catch the working yarn with your hook and pull a loop through to the front, leaving both working yarn and a tail on the wrong side. Continue to insert your hook, catch the working yarn from beneath, and pull the yarn through the loop until your design is completed. Fasten off and weave in the ends. Your surface crochet will be shaped by where you place your hook.

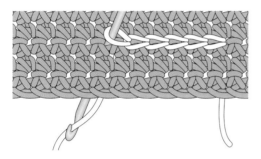

WEAVING IN ENDS

To finish your work nicely, you'll want to weave in the ends after fastening off. To do so, thread the tail (the cut end of the yarn) through a tapestry needle, and weave the needle through a few stitches on the wrong side of the work.

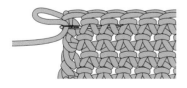

After about an inch, weave the tail in the opposite direction so that the yarn won't come out after handling. Snip the end so that the yarn doesn't show.

For pieces that are stuffed, you can simply pull the ends to the wrong side of the work to hide them.

ASSEMBLY TECHNIQUES

Many of the projects in this book are crocheted in pieces that are later assembled into the finished piece. The following techniques will help you tackle the job of assembly with ease.

Mattress Stitch

The mattress stitch is used when you're attaching two strips of crochet fabric together along the edges of the work. This provides a nearly invisible seam that makes the piece appear as if it were crocheted in one piece.

To attach two pieces together using the mattress stitch, thread the long tail of one piece through a tapestry needle. Catch two loops on the side of one piece by running the tapestry needle through the turning chains (see page 10), and then through two loops at the adjacent place on the second piece. Take the needle back to the first piece, moving up to the next row, and repeat.

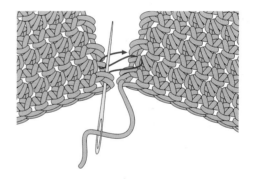

Continue zigzagging in this manner, occasionally pulling the yarn taut, until both pieces have been attached. To finish, tie a knot (I use a square knot, but any knot will do) and weave in the end.

Running Stitch

The running stitch is used to attach an appliqué onto a background piece. The advantage of the running stitch over the whipstitch is that the running stitch encourages the appliqué to lie flat against the background.

To attach two pieces together using the running stitch, thread the long tail of the appliqué through a tapestry needle. Insert the tapestry needle straight through both the appliqué and background so that it comes out the wrong side of the background piece.

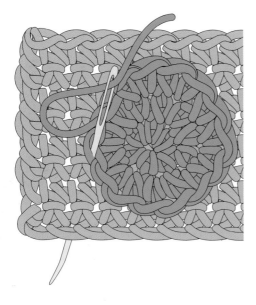

Pull the tapestry needle so that the yarn is taut. A fraction of an inch from where the yarn is currently threaded through the background piece, insert your needle through the background and appliqué, pulling through to the top.

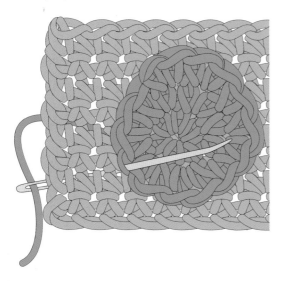

Continue in this manner until the entire appliqué is attached. To finish, tie a knot and weave in the end.

Whipstitch

The whipstitch is the default technique used when attaching two pieces together: it's easy and results in a stitch that isn't very noticeable.

To attach a piece to a background (such as attaching a snout to a bear), thread the long tail through a tapestry needle. Insert the needle through one stitch on the background piece and through the back loop of one stitch on the piece you're attaching. Continue stitching in this manner until you've completely attached your piece.

Joining to background

To attach two pieces together along the edges (such as joining two halves of a pillow or stitching together blanket medallions), thread the long tail through a tapestry needle. With stitches aligned, insert the needle into the back loop of each piece and pull the yarn through. Repeat to end. To finish your whipstitching, tie a knot, and weave in the end.

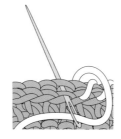

Joining pieces
along an edge

Joining medallions

ADDITIONAL TECHNIQUES

BOLD AND BRIGHT

Every baby has the makings of a tiny artist. The ultimate inspiration? Surround your little one with a piece of art, in crocheted form! This afghan is constructed in vertical strips that are sewn together. It's an easy way to stitch a color-blocked piece without a lot of fancy color work.

SKILL LEVEL: Easy

SIZE: 31" x 38", blocked

GAUGE

16 sts x 20 rows of sc = 4" square

MATERIALS

Yarns

220 Superwash from Cascade (100% superwash wool; 3.5 oz; 220 yds) (4)

- **MC** 2 skeins in color 910A Winter White
- **A** 2 skeins in color 1913 Jet
- **B** 1 skein in color 848 Blueberry
- **C** 1 skein in color 824 Yellow
- **D** 1 skein in color 809 Really Red

Hooks and Notions

Size H-8 (5 mm) crochet hook

Crocheter's toolbox supplies (see page 8)

PATTERN NOTE

Cut yarn at end of every color block.

COLOR-BLOCKED STRIPS

Make 4. Instructions are for strip 1 with colors and stitch counts for strips (2, 3, 4) following in parentheses. Where just one color appears, it applies to all strips.

With MC (MC, MC, C), ch 21 (17, 49, 25).

Row 1: Sc in 2nd ch from hook, and each st across. 20 (16, 48, 24) sts

Rows 2–60: Ch 1, turn, sc in each st across.

Rows 61–66: With A, ch 1, turn, sc in each st across.

Rows 67–92: With MC (D, MC, MC), ch 1, turn, sc in each st across.

Rows 93–98: With A, ch 1, turn, sc in each st across.

Rows 99–128: With MC (MC, B, MC), ch 1, turn, sc in each st across.

Rows 129–134: With A, ch 1, turn, sc in each st across.

Rows 135–184: With B (C, D, MC), ch 1, turn, sc in each st across.

Fasten off.

BLACK STRIPS

Make 3.

With A, ch 6.

Row 1: Sc in 2nd ch from hook, and in each st across. 5 sts

Rows 2–184: Ch 1, turn, sc in each st across.

Fasten off.

ASSEMBLY

Block pieces (see page 77) to schematic measurements below. With A and tapestry needle, use mattress stitch (see page 15) to sew each strip together.

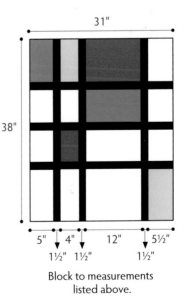

Block to measurements listed above.

Primary Planet Mobile

As children, we learn that planets are balls, orbiting around the solar system in ways that still seem magical. I designed this mobile so that even the tiniest among us can glance upward and experience the awe of some seemingly magical orbs!

SKILL LEVEL: Easy

SIZE: Approx 10" diameter

GAUGE

Large ball at end of rnd 8 = 4"- diameter circle

MATERIALS

Yarns

Vickie Howell Sheep(ish) from Bernat (70% acrylic, 30% wool; 3 oz; 167 yds) (4)

> A 80 yards in color 15 Red(ish)
>
> B 75 yards in color 16 Teal(ish)
>
> C 50 yards in color 12 Yellow(ish)

Hooks and Notions

Size H-8 (5 mm) crochet hook

Crocheter's toolbox supplies (see page 8)

Two 4"-diameter Styrofoam balls

Four 2½"-diameter Styrofoam balls

10" embroidery hoop (spring closure optional)

10 yards of ⅛"-wide ribbon

1" metal key ring

Craft glue

PATTERN NOTE

Work through back loops only.

BALLS

Make 6: 1 large, 1 small in blue; 1 large, 1 small in red; 2 small in yellow.

With selected color, ch 2.

Both Sizes

Rnd 1: Sc 6 times in 2nd ch from hook. 6 sts

Rnd 2: Sc twice in each st. 12 sts

Rnd 3: (Sc twice in next st, sc in next st) 6 times. 18 sts

Rnd 4: (Sc twice in next st, sc in next 2 sts) 6 times. 24 sts

Rnd 5: (Sc twice in next st, sc in next 3 sts) 6 times. 30 sts

Small Only

Rnds 6–11: Sc in each st.

Skip to "Both Sizes Back Together Now" on page 22.

Large Only

Rnd 6: (Sc twice in next st, sc in next 4 sts) 6 times. 36 sts

Rnd 7: (Sc twice in next st, sc in next 5 sts) 6 times. 42 sts

Rnd 8: (Sc twice in next st, sc in next 6 sts) 6 times. 48 sts

Rnds 9–17: Sc in each st.

Rnd 18: (Sc2tog, sc in next 6 sts) 6 times. 42 sts

Rnd 19: (Sc2tog, sc in next 5 sts) 6 times. 36 sts

Rnd 20: (Sc2tog, sc in next 4 sts) 6 times. 30 sts

Need Better Fit?

Are you in a pickle because your stitched piece isn't at the ball's midpoint? You can adjust to fit by adding a work-even round (see rounds 6–11 for small or 9–17 for large) or ripping out a round of crochet stitches.

Both Sizes Back Together Now

Insert Styrofoam ball into your crocheted piece.

Rnd 12 (21): (Sc2tog, sc in next 3 sts) 6 times. 24 sts

Rnd 13 (22): (Sc2tog, sc in next 2 sts) 6 times. 18 sts

Rnd 14 (23): (Sc2tog, sc in next st) 6 times. 12 sts

Rnd 15 (24): (Sc2tog) 6 times. 6 sts

Rnd 16 (25): Sl st in next and 4th sts tog, rem sts unworked.

Fasten off, pulling tail to inside.

ASSEMBLY

Separate embroidery hoop into 2 parts.

Cut 3 lengths of ribbon, each 24" long. Run each length through the ring (used to hang mobile), gluing end of each one in place and evenly spaced along outer embroidery hoop (see photo at left, top).

Cut remaining ribbon into 6 assorted lengths. Loop one end of each length around inner embroidery hoop, and attach other end to a ball by tying a bow.

Assemble embroidery hoop, adjusting optional screw for fit, and wrap A around both halves. Completely surround the hoop and glue start and end in place.

Zabby the Giggle Monster

Children are prone to what we adults call silliness: the propensity to giggle at any opportunity. I designed Zabby because I wanted to catch that gigglyness in crochet form: googly eyes, a hypnotizing tummy, and a crazy triangle shape. She'll eek a giggle out of anyone!

SKILL LEVEL: Easy

SIZE: Approx 7½" tall, stuffed

GAUGE

Body at end of rnd 5 = 2½"-diameter circle

MATERIALS

Yarns

Simply Soft from Caron (100% acrylic; 6 oz; 315 yds) (4)

- **MC** 130 yards in color 9759 Ocean
- **A** 5 yards in color 9701 White
- **B** 5 yards in color 9727 Black
- **C** 5 yards in color 0730 Autumn Red
- **D** 5 yards in color 9755 Sunshine

Hooks and Notions

Size H-8 (5 mm) crochet hook

Crocheter's toolbox supplies (see page 8)

Polyester stuffing

PATTERN NOTE

Work through back loops only.

BODY

With MC, ch 2.

Rnd 1: Sc 6 times in 2nd ch from hook. 6 sts

Rnd 2: Sc twice in each st. 12 sts

Rnd 3: (Sc twice in next st, sc in next st) 6 times. 18 sts

Rnd 4: (Sc twice in next st, sc in next 2 sts) 6 times. 24 sts

Rnd 5: (Sc twice in next st, sc in next 3 sts) 6 times. 30 sts

Rnd 6: Sc in each st.

Rnd 7: (Sc twice in next st, sc in next 4 sts) 6 times. 36 sts

Rnd 8: Sc in each st.

Rnd 9: (Sc twice in next st, sc in next 5 sts) 6 times. 42 sts

Rnd 10: Sc in each st.

Rnd 11: (Sc twice in next st, sc in next 6 sts) 6 times. 48 sts

Rnd 12: Sc in each st.

Rnds 13–28: Cont working rnds in patt as established, working a rnd of 6 evenly spaced inc followed by a rnd without inc at end of rnd 28. 96 sts total

Rnd 29: Sc in each st.

Fasten off.

BACKBONE

With MC, ch 13.

Row 1: Turn, sc in 2nd ch from hook and each st across. 12 sts

Rows 2–36: Sc in each st across.

Fasten off with long tail.

EYE

Make 2.

With A, ch 2.

Rnd 1: Sc 6 times in 2nd ch from hook. 6 sts

Rnd 2: Sc twice in each st around. 12 sts

Rnd 3: (Sc twice in next st, sc in next st) 6 times. 18 sts

Fasten off with long tail.

PUPIL

Make 2.

With B, ch 2.

Rnd 1: Sc 6 times in 2nd ch from hook. 6 sts

Fasten off with long tail.

ARM

Make 2.

With MC, ch 2.

Rnd 1: Sc 6 times in 2nd ch from hook. 6 sts

Rnd 2: Sc twice in each st. 12 sts

Rnd 3: (Sc twice in next st, sc in next st) 6 times. 18 sts

Rnds 4–6: Sc in each st.

Rnd 7: (Sc2tog, sc in next st) 6 times. 12 sts

Rnds 8–12: Sc in each st.

Fasten off with long tail.

FOOT

Make 2.

With MC, ch 2.

Rnd 1: Sc 6 times in 2nd ch from hook. 6 sts

Rnd 2: Sc twice in each st. 12 sts

Rnd 3: (Sc twice in next st, sc in next st) 6 times. 18 sts

Rnds 4 and 5: Sc in each st.

Fasten off with long tail.

TUMMY

With C, ch 2.

Rnd 1: Sc 6 times in 2nd ch from hook. 6 sts

Rnd 2: With D, ch 1, sc twice in each st, sl st in ch at start of rnd. 12 sts

Rnd 3: With C, ch 1, (sc twice in next st, sc in next st) 6 times, sl st in ch at start of rnd. 18 sts

Rnd 4: With D, ch 1, (sc twice in next st, sc in next 2 sts) 6 times, sl st in ch at start of rnd. 24 sts

Rnd 5: With C, ch 1, (sc twice in next st, sc in next 3 sts) 6 times, sl st in ch at start of rnd. 30 sts

Rnd 6: With D, ch 1, (sc twice in next st, sc in next 4 sts) 6 times, sl st in ch at start of rnd. 36 sts

Fasten off with long tail.

Why the "Ch 1"?

You may have noticed that the tummy rounds contain a *ch 1* and *sl st,* which are missing from the rest of the pattern. This is called *working in joined rounds* (as opposed to the *spiral rounds* present in the rest of the pattern). Joined rounds make the color changes on the tummy nice and clean!

ASSEMBLY

Use the whipstitch (see page 16) to attach the pieces on Zabby, unless otherwise specified. Use the long tail to attach each piece.

Attach backbone along final rnd of body. Attaching one side of

backbone should consume 36 sts of final body rnd and 12 sts along foundation chain. Stuff body once 3 sides of backbone have been attached, and then attach final side.

This monster has a funny shape! Be sure to sew her together so that she looks like a triangle from the side, with the backbone along the back, as shown above.

Stuff feet and attach at bottom of monster, along rnds 5–12. Stuff arms. Flatten and attach along rnds 20–22 of body, one on each side.

Attach tummy to front of body, at rnds 6–20. With B, embroider mouth as a straight line above tummy. With A and 3 stitches, embroider a small tooth.

Using running stitch (see page 15), attach pupils to eyes, askew so that they will appear to be googly. Attach eyes to body at rnds 22–27.

Funky Argyle Pillow

This pillow is the perfect mate to the Funky Argyle Afghan (page 31). If you're nervous about color work, I recommend starting with this piece, and then moving on to the afghan once you've hit your stride.

This big, cuddly pillow is wonderfully suited for mommy and baby to use for resting or snuggling.

SKILL LEVEL: Intermediate

SIZE: 14" x 28", blocked and stuffed

GAUGE

14 sts x 18 rows of sc = 4" square

MATERIALS

Yarns
Simply Soft from Caron (100% acrylic; 6 oz; 315 yds) 【4】

    MC 530 yards in color 9701 White

    CC1 175 yards in color 9607 Limelight

    CC2 175 yards in color 9608 Blue Mint

    CC3 25 yards in color 9605 Mango

Hooks and Notions
Size H-8 (5 mm) crochet hook

Crocheter's toolbox supplies (see page 8)

14" x 28" pillow form

PATTERN NOTES

Crochet in large blocks of color using intarsia technique (see "A Note about Intarsia," right).

For clean color changes reference "Changing Colors" on page 14.

Diagonal lines are obtained by the surface-crochet technique (see page 15).

A Note about Intarsia

Because the colors are worked in large blocks, working with only two balls of yarn is impractical.

I recommend the intarsia technique, which is a fancy word for saying "use a new ball of yarn for each block of color."

While crocheting, you'll need to juggle a number of balls (as illustrated below), but the result is a professional-looking piece with almost no strands carried on the wrong side.

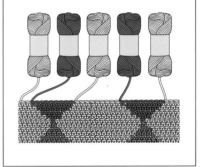

PILLOW SIDES

Make 2.

With MC, ch 104.

Row 1: Turn, sc in 2nd ch from hook and each st across. 103 sts

Row 2: Ch 1, turn, with MC, sc in 6 sts, following center section of

Funky Argyle Chart (page 29) and using CC1 as contrast color, sc in each st, changing color as indicated on chart for 3 reps; with MC, sc in rem 7 sts.

Row 3: Ch 1, turn, with MC, sc 7 sts for edge, follow same chart but right to left, sc in each st, changing color as indicated for 3 reps; with MC, sc in rem 6 edge sts.

Rows 4–31: Keeping edge sts in MC as established, work rows 4–31 of chart center repeat section.

Rows 32–63: Ch 1, turn, work edge sts in MC as established, follow center section of chart and using CC2 as the contrast color, changing colors as indicated on chart.

Fasten off.

DIAGONAL LINES AND FINISHING

Block your pillow sides (see page 77) to schematic measurements at right.

With CC3, work surface crochet (see page 15) diagonal lines across.

Beg in center of each white base triangle and in corners of pillow, surface crochet at 45° angle across piece, with diagonal lines crossing in the center of each diamond. Use diagram at right as reference. Weave in ends.

Holding WS together and with length of MC, whipstitch (see page 16) around edges of 3 sides. Insert pillow form, then close up final side.

Chart Reading 101

Charts don't need to be scary! Even though the chart on page 29 may send your heart racing, this is actually a really great first-time chart-reading project, since the design is a not-too-tricky diamond.

Each square represents a stitch. The key with the chart tells you that they're all single crochet stitches and shows you the color to use for the stitch. You're on row 2 when you start the chart, so you *read* the chart from left to right. Crochet the six edge stitches specified in the row 2 instructions, then make your first *repeat* of 30 stitches (the middle, large portion of the chart): that's 15 stitches in MC, 1 stitch in CC1, and then 14 stitches in MC. It's the start of your first diamond! To start your second diamond go back to the start of row 2 and begin reading the chart again, from left to right.

When you've finished all three of your repeats for the row, make the remaining stitches in MC (as instructed) to complete the row.

And remember, when you do your next row, you'll read your chart from right to left because you've turned your work around! Ignore the skinny columns at both sides of the larger center portion of the chart. Those are the edge stitches for the Funky Argyle Afghan.

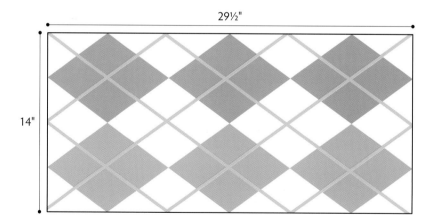

29½"

14"

Funky Argyle Chart

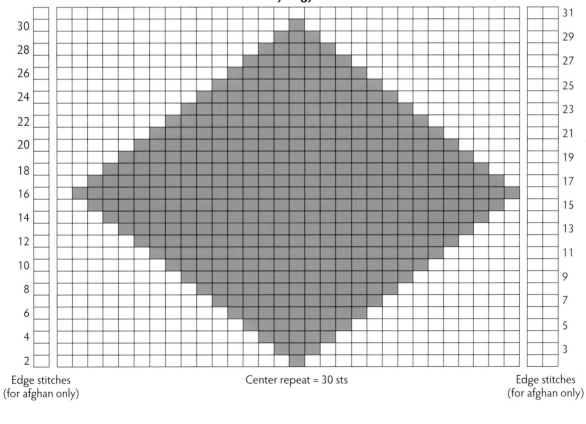

Edge stitches
(for afghan only)

Center repeat = 30 sts

Edge stitches
(for afghan only)

Legend

☐ Sc in MC

▨ Sc in CC1 or CC2

Funky Argyle Afghan

I adore bold and bright colors. My favorite combination is lime green, turquoise, and orange. While mulling over how to sneak my favorite color combo into this book, it suddenly struck me that they'd look absolutely breathtaking in an old-fashioned pattern like argyle. The old made new—I love it!

This afghan is worked in a fairly simple color work pattern, with the diagonal stitches applied at the end using the surface crochet technique.

SKILL LEVEL: Intermediate

SIZE: 30¼" x 35"

GAUGE

14 sts x 18 rows of sc = 4" square

MATERIALS

Yarns

Sweater from Spud and Chloe (superwash 55% wool, 45% organic cotton; 3.5 oz; 160 yds) (4)

    MC 4 skeins in color 7517 Igloo

    CC1 3 skeins in color 7502 Grass

    CC2 2 skeins in color 7510 Splash

    CC3 1 skein in color 7508 Pollen

Hooks and Notions

Size H-8 (5 mm) crochet hook

Crocheter's toolbox supplies (see page 8)

PATTERN NOTES

Crochet in large blocks of color using intarsia technique (see "A Note about Intarsia" on page 27).

For clean color changes, refer to "Changing Colors" on page 14.

Diagonal lines are surface crochet (see page 15).

AFGHAN

With MC, ch 124.

Row 1: Turn, sc in 2nd ch from hook and each st across. 123 sts

Rows 2–31: Ch 1, turn, work Funky Argyle Chart including edge sts (see page 29) using CC1 as the contrast color and changing colors as indicated on the chart for a total of 4 center-section reps.

Rows 32–63: Ch 1, turn, rep rows 2–31 using CC2 as contrast color.

Rows 64–105: Rep rows 2–63.

Rows 106–136: Rep rows 2–31 once.

Fasten off.

DIAGONAL LINES AND FINISHING

Block your afghan (see page 77) to schematic measurements.

With CC3, work diagonal lines using surface crochet. Beg in center of each white base triangle and in corners of afghan, work surface crochet at 45° angle across piece, with diagonal lines crossing in the center of each diamond. Use diagram below as reference. Weave in ends.

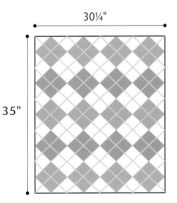

I'll admit it: I don't really like calling this a granny-square pattern—there's nothing granny about it! Regardless, this is your classic granny square, but in fun colors that give the blanket a totally modern look. Since this blanket is crocheted in squares, it's the perfect portable project. Want it larger? Just add more squares!

SKILL LEVEL: Easy

SIZE: 36" x 43", blocked

GAUGE

Square = 6" x 6", before blocking

MATERIALS

Yarns

Vickie Howell Sheep(ish) from Bernat (70% acrylic, 30% wool; 3 oz; 167 yds) **(4)**

- **MC** 3 skeins in color 2 Gun Metal(ish)
- **A** 2 skeins in color 20 Chartreuse(ish)
- **B** 2 skeins in color 12 Yellow(ish)
- **C** 2 skeins in color 16 Teal(ish)
- **D** 1 skein in color 15 Red(ish)
- **E** 1 skein in color 6 Magenta(ish)

Hooks and Notions

Size H-8 (5 mm) crochet hook

Crocheter's toolbox supplies (see page 8)

SQUARES

Make 30: 3 of D, 7 of B, 10 of A, 7 of C, and 3 of E.

Foundation ring: With selected color (A, B, C, D, or E), ch 6, sl st in first ch (to form ring).

Rnd 1: Ch 3 (ch 3 counts as dc), dc twice in center of ring, (ch 3, dc 3 times into center of ring) 3 times, ch 3, sl st into 3rd ch at start of rnd. 4 groups of 3 dc

Rnd 2: Sl st in next 2 sts, then sl st into next ch-3 sp, ch 3, dc twice into same sp, ch 3, dc 3 times into same sp, (ch 1, dc 3 times into next ch-3 sp, ch 3, dc 3 times into same sp) 3 times, ch 1, sl st into 3rd ch at start of rnd. 8 groups of 3 dc

Rnd 3: Sl st in next 2 sts, then sl st into next ch-3 sp, ch 3, dc twice into same sp, ch 3, dc 3 times into same sp, (ch 1, dc 3 times into next ch-1 sp, ch 1, dc 3 times into next ch-3 sp, ch 3, dc 3 times into same sp) 3 times, ch 1, dc 3 times into next ch-1 sp, ch 1, sl st into 3rd ch at start of rnd. 12 groups of 3 dc

Rnd 4: Sl st in next 2 sts, then sl st into next ch-3 sp, ch 3, dc twice into same sp, ch 3, dc 3 times into same sp, *(ch 1, dc 3 times into next ch-1 sp) twice, ch 1, dc 3 times into next ch-3 sp, ch 3, dc 3 times into same sp; rep from * 3 times, (ch 1, dc 3 times into next ch-1 sp) twice, ch 1, sl st into 3rd ch at start of rnd. 16 groups of 3 dc

Rnd 5: Sl st in next 2 sts, then sl st into next ch-3 sp, ch 3, dc twice into same sp, ch 3, dc 3 times into same sp, *(ch 1, dc 3 times into next ch-1 sp) 3 times, ch 1, dc 3 times into next ch-3 sp, ch 3, dc 3 times into same sp; rep from * 3 times, (ch 1, dc 3 times into next ch-1 sp) 3 times, ch 1, sl st into 3rd ch at start of rnd. 20 groups of 3 dc

Rnd 6: With MC, sl st in next 2 sts, sl st into next ch-3 sp, ch 3, dc twice into same sp, ch 3, dc 3 times into same sp, *(ch 1, dc 3 times into next ch-1 sp) 4 times, ch 1, dc 3 times into next ch-3 sp, ch 3, dc 3 times into same sp; rep from * 3 times, (ch 1, dc 3 times into next ch-1 sp) 4 times, ch 1, sl st into 3rd ch at start of rnd. 24 groups of 3 dc

Fasten off with 24"-long tail.

ASSEMBLY AND FINISHING

Block each square (see page 77) to 7" x 7".

Arrange squares as shown in diagram below. Using long tail from each square, whipstitch (see page 16) squares tog, working through bl of each st.

To crochet a border, join MC with sl st in bl of any outer stitch, ch 1, sc bl in each st around entire afghan, sl st in first ch and fasten off.

Weave in ends.

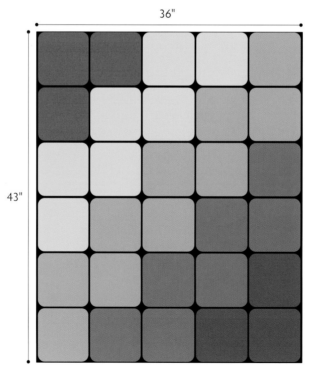

36"

43"

●●●●● Colorful Wiggle Pillow

There's something about combining the bright colors of a rainbow with gray that gets me. It's just so awesome. This pillow features a whimsical wiggle stitch, which is really just double crochet stitches grouped together in an interesting way. The back of this pillow features rainbow stripes, so the pillow is reversible and exciting no matter how you look at it!

SKILL LEVEL: Experienced

SIZE: 16" square, stuffed

GAUGE

14 sts x 8 rows of dc = 4" square

MATERIALS

Yarns

Sweater from Spud and Chloe (superwash 55% wool, 45% organic cotton; 3.5 oz; 160 yds) ▒▒

> **MC** 160 yards in color 7521 Beluga
>
> **A** 95 yards in color 7518 Barn
>
> **B** 95 yards in color 7508 Pollen
>
> **C** 95 yards in color 7505 Firefly
>
> **D** 95 yards in color 7502 Grass
>
> **E** 95 yards in color 7510 Splash
>
> **F** 95 yards in color 7523 Lilac

Hooks and Notions

Size H-8 (5 mm) crochet hook

Crocheter's toolbox supplies (see page 8)

16" square pillow form

PATTERN NOTE

The back has more stitches than the front to compensate for the stretching that the wiggle stitch causes on the front.

FRONT

With MC, ch 52.

Row 1: Dc in 4th ch from hook and each st across (ch 3 counts as dc). 50 dc

Rows 2–5: Ch 3, turn, dc in next st and each st across.

Row 6: With A, ch 3, turn, dc in next st and each st across.

Row 7: Ch 3, rotate piece so top edge is on your right, dc 2 around tch at end of row, *dc 1 bet current and next st at base of row (indicated by arrow).

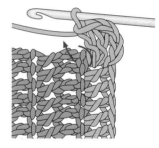

Rotate piece so top edge is on your left, and dc 3 around next dc post (indicated by arrow).

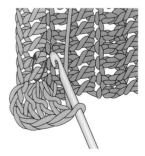

COLORFUL WIGGLE PILLOW

Dc 1 bet current st and next st at top of row (indicated by arrow).

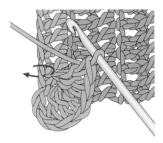

Rotate piece so top edge is on your right, and dc 3 around next dc post (indicated by arrow).

Rep from * to end to last st, dc bet current st and tch at base of row, dc 3 around tch, sl st in top of same tch.

Rows 8 and 9: Rep rows 6 and 7.

Rows 10 and 11: With MC, ch 3, turn, dc in next st and each st across.

Rows 12–41: Rep rows 6–11, replacing A with B, C, D, E, and F (in that order).

Rows 42–46: With MC, ch 3, turn, dc in next st and each st across.

Fasten off.

BACK

With A, ch 55.

Row 1: Dc in 4th ch from hook (ch 3 counts as dc) and each st across. 53 dc

Rows 2–5: Ch 3, turn, dc in next st and each st across. 53 dc

Rows 6–10: With B, ch 3, turn, dc in next st and each st across. 53 dc

Rows 11–30: Rep rows 6–10, replacing B with C, D, E, and F (in that order).

Fasten off.

ASSEMBLY

Place WS of front and back tog. With MC, whipstitch (see page 16) around edges. Insert pillow form after 3 edges have been stitched, and complete the 4th edge.

Weave in end.

Wiggles and Posts

The wiggle stitch is a funny one. You work a row of double crochet stitches, and then on the surface you crochet around these stitches using the same technique as the front-post double crochet stitch (see page 12).

Rainbow Bunting

Nothing's more glorious than a rainbow appearing in the sky after a rainstorm. Rainbows are so fantastic, partially because they are so fleeting. No more! I designed this bunting so that you can bring the colors and joy of a rainbow inside to your little one's nursery.

SKILL LEVEL: Easy

SIZE: 6" per side, before blocking

GAUGE

8 rnds in sc = 4"-diameter circle

MATERIALS

Yarns

220 Superwash from Cascade (100% superwash wool; 3.5 oz; 220 yds) (4)

- **A** 55 yards in color 1921 Persimmon
- **B** 55 yards in color 821 Daffodil
- **C** 55 yards in color 824 Yellow
- **D** 55 yards in color 802 Green Apple
- **E** 55 yards in color 812 Turquoise
- **F** 55 yards in color 804 Amethyst
- **G** 25 yards in color 816 Gray

Hooks and Notions

Size H-8 (5 mm) crochet hook

Crocheter's toolbox supplies (see page 8)

PATTERN NOTE

Work through back loops only.

TRIANGLES

Make 2 in *each* color A, B, C, D, E, and F.

With specified color, ch 2.

Rnd 1: Sc 6 times in 2nd ch from hook. 6 sts

Rnd 2: (Sc 3 times in next st, sc in next st) 3 times. 12 sts

Rnd 3: Sc in next st, (sc 3 times in next st, sc in next 3 sts) 2 times, sc 3 times in next st, sc in next 2 sts. 18 sts

Rnd 4: Sc in next 2 sts, (sc 3 times in next st, sc in next 5 sts) 2 times, sc 3 times in next st, sc in next 3 sts. 24 sts

Rnd 5: Sc in next 3 sts, (sc 3 times in next st, sc in next 7 sts) 2 times, sc 3 times in next st, sc in next 4 sts. 30 sts

Cont working rnds in patt as established, working 3 sc in center st of each corner and 2 more sc on each side of triangle until each side has 23 sts, for 13 rnds. 78 sts total

Fasten off with long tail.

RIBBON

With gray, ch 401.

Row 1: Turn, sc in 2nd ch from hook and each ch across. 400 sts Fasten off.

ASSEMBLY

Using st markers, position triangles along main ribbon so that they're evenly spaced, leaving approx 6" of empty ribbon on each side. Holding WS tog and using long tail and running stitch (see page 15), stitch tog both triangles of the same color. When working 3rd side, include main ribbon bet triangles when stitching to attach.

Weave in ends.

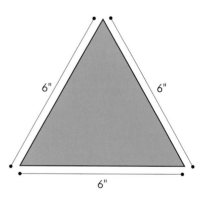

Personalized Bunting

Want a more personalized touch? With any stitch you like, embroider each triangle with a letter of your little one's name! Feel free to crochet more (or fewer) triangles as needed to fit the baby's name. Simply space them evenly along the ribbon, and you have a unique name banner!

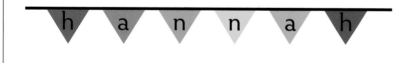

PRETTY IN PASTEL

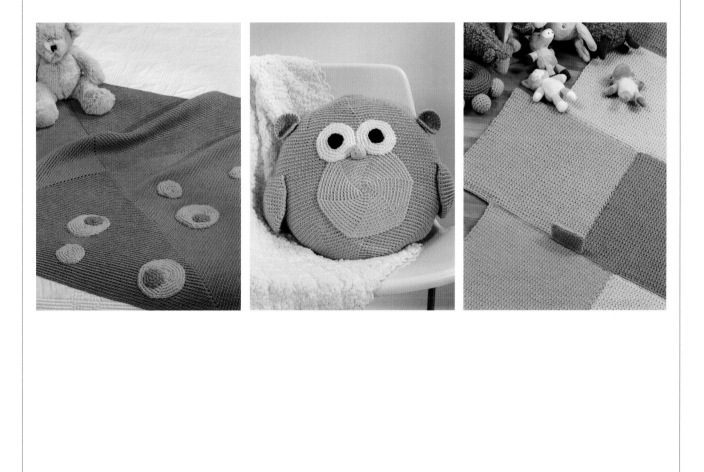

●●●● Pastel Petals Afghan

Who wouldn't want to be cuddled in a cascade of scallops in pastel colors? The design for this afghan was inspired by a flower that only exists in my imagination, colorful and relentlessly blossoming! This chunky blanket is a quick project that looks fabulous in any color combination.

SKILL LEVEL: Easy

SIZE: 39" diameter, blocked

GAUGE

Afghan at end of rnd 4 = 2½"-diameter circle, blocked

MATERIALS

Yarns

Baby's First from Lion Brand (55% acrylic, 45% cotton; 3.5 oz; 120 yds) ●5●

A 1 skein in color 925-156 Beanstalk

B 2 skeins in color 925-106 Splish Splash

C 2 skeins in color 925-099 Pixie Dust

D 3 skeins in color 925-101 Twinkle Toes

E 3 skeins in color 925-100 Cotton Ball

Hooks and Notions

Size K-10½ (6.5 mm) crochet hook

Crocheter's toolbox supplies (see page 8)

PATTERN NOTE

Work through back loops only unless otherwise indicated.

AFGHAN

With A, ch 2.

Rnd 1: Sc 6 times in 2nd ch from hook. 6 sts

Rnd 2: Sc twice in each st. 12 sts

Rnd 3: (Sc twice in next st, sc in next st) 6 times. 18 sts

Rnd 4: (Sc twice in next st, sc in next 2 sts) 6 times. 24 sts

Rnd 5: (Sc twice in next st, sc in next 3 sts) 6 times. 30 sts

Rnd 6: (Sc twice in next st, sc in next 4 sts) 6 times. 36 sts

Rnd 7: (Sc twice in next st, sc in next 5 sts) 6 times. 42 sts

Rnd 8: (Sc twice in next st, sc in next 6 sts) 6 times. 48 sts

Rnds 9–15: Cont working rnds in patt as established, working 6 evenly spaced inc every rnd. 90 sts at end of rnd 15

Cont in patt as established working 15 rnds *each* in color B, then C, D, and E. 450 sts total

Fasten off.

SCALLOP EDGING

Crochet scallop edge through fl of final round of each color.

Scallop Edging for First Circle

Join A with sl st to any st in rnd 15 (final rnd of A).

*Sk 1, dc 5 times in next st, sk 1, sl st in next st; rep from * around entire rnd. On final rep (may not be a complete rep) sl st in first st (instead of st on same rnd) to join in circle. Fasten off.

Remaining Color Edgings

Crochet the scallop edging on each of the remaining circles, but instead use B to crochet the edging on the last round of the B circle, use C to crochet the edging on the last round of the C circle, and match D and E in the same way. Weave in ends. Block (see page 77) to schematic measurements below.

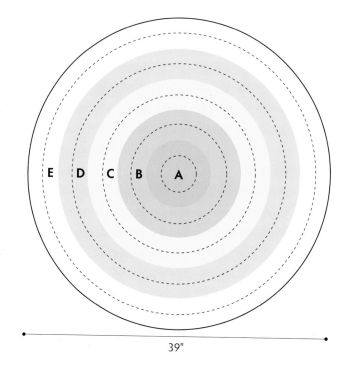

39"

Whoooo can resist an adorable owl, especially one that doubles as a pillow? I certainly can't. I adore owls! Crochet up this owlish cutie, and be sure to make his tummy in a color that coordinates with your nursery's color scheme. He'll be an irresistible addition.

SKILL LEVEL: Easy

SIZE: 14" tall, stuffed

GAUGE

Body at end of rnd 8 = 4"-diameter circle

MATERIALS

Yarns

Simply Soft from Caron (100% acrylic; 6 oz; 315 yds) ④

MC 2 skeins in color 9703 Bone

A 40 yards in color 9712 Soft Blue

B 10 yards in color 9701 White

C 5 yards in color 9727 Black

D 5 yards in color 9755 Sunshine

Hooks and Notions

Size H-8 (5 mm) crochet hook

14"-diameter pillow form

Crocheter's toolbox supplies (see page 8)

1" polyester stuffing (approx size of cotton ball)

PATTERN NOTE

Work through back loops only.

BODY

With MC, ch 2.

Rnd 1: Sc 6 times in 2nd ch from hook. 6 sts

Rnd 2: Sc twice in each st. 12 sts

Rnd 3: (Sc twice in next st, sc in next st) 6 times. 18 sts

Rnd 4: (Sc twice in next st, sc in next 2 sts) 6 times. 24 sts

Rnd 5: (Sc twice in next st, sc in next 3 sts) 6 times. 30 sts

Rnd 6: (Sc twice in next st, sc in next 4 sts) 6 times. 36 sts

Rnd 7: (Sc twice in next st, sc in next 5 sts) 6 times. 42 sts

Rnd 8: (Sc twice in next st, sc in next 6 sts) 6 times. 48 sts

Rnds 9–19: Cont working rnds in patt as established, working 6 evenly spaced inc every rnd. 114 sts total at end of rnd 19

Rnds 20–59: Sc in each st.

Insert pillow form into work. Cont to crochet, enclosing form.

Rnd 60: (Sc2tog, sc in next 17 sts) 6 times. 108 sts

Rnd 61: (Sc2tog, sc in next 16 sts) 6 times. 102 sts

Rnd 62: (Sc2tog, sc in next 15 sts) 6 times. 96 sts

Rnd 63: (Sc2tog, sc in next 14 sts) 6 times. 90 sts

Rnds 64–77: Cont working rnds in patt as established, working 6 evenly spaced dec every rnd. 6 sts at end of rnd 77

Rnd 78: Sc next and 4th sts tog, rem sts unworked. 1 st

Fasten off.

WINGS

Make 2.

With MC, ch 2.

Rnd 1: Sc 6 times in 2nd ch from hook. 6 sts

Rnd 2: Sc twice in each st. 12 sts

Rnd 3: (Sc twice in next st, sc in next st) 6 times. 18 sts

Rnd 4: (Sc twice in next st, sc in next 2 sts) 6 times. 24 sts

Rnd 5: (Sc twice in next st, sc in next 3 sts) 6 times. 30 sts

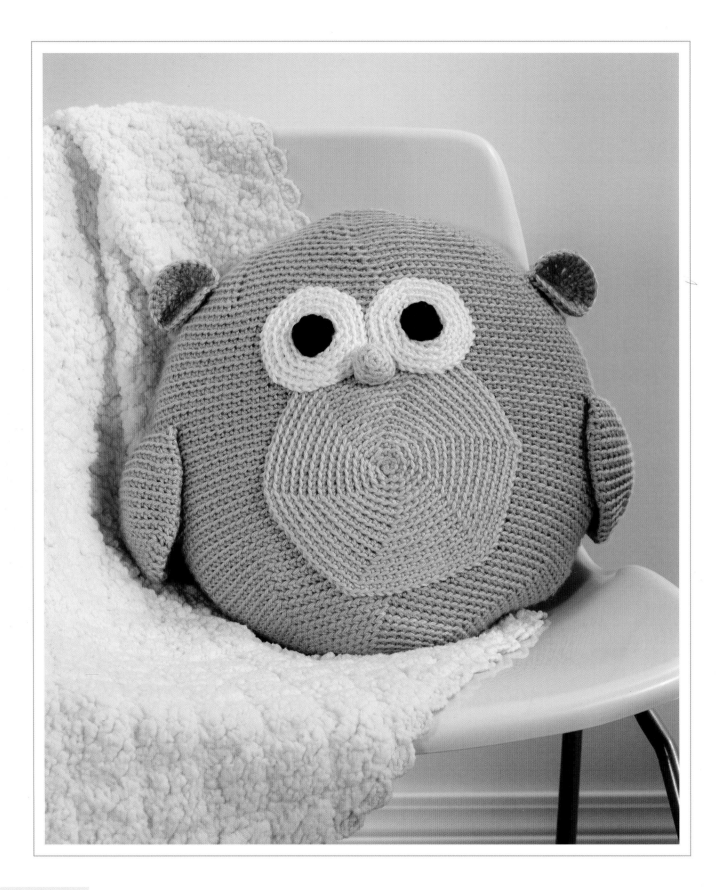

OAKLEY THE OWL

Rnd 6: (Sc twice in next st, sc in next 4 sts) 6 times. 36 sts

Rnd 7: (Sc twice in next st, sc in next 5 sts) 6 times. 42 sts

Rnd 8: (Sc twice in next st, sc in next 6 sts) 6 times. 48 sts

Rnds 9–14: Sc in each st around.

Rnd 15: (Sc2tog, sc in next 6 sts) 6 times. 42 sts

Rnd 16: (Sc2tog, sc in next 5 sts) 6 times. 36 sts

Rnd 17: (Sc2tog, sc in next 4 sts) 6 times. 30 sts

Fasten off with long tail.

TUMMY

With A, ch 2.

Work first 15 rnds of body (see page 45).

Fasten off with long tail.

EYE

With B, ch 2.

Work rnds 1–6 of body.

Fasten off with long tail.

PUPIL

Make 2.

With C, ch 2.

Work rnds 1–6 of body.

Fasten off with long tail.

BEAK

With D, ch 2.

Rnd 1: Sc 6 times in 2nd ch from hook. 6 sts

Rnd 2: Sc twice in each st. 12 sts

Rnd 3: Sc in each st.

Fasten off with long tail.

EAR

Make 2.

With MC, ch 4.

Row 1: Dc 5 times in 4th ch from hook (ch 3 counts as dc). 6 dc

Rows 2 and 3: Ch 3, turn, dc in first dc, dc twice in each st across. 24 dc on row 3

Fasten off with long tail.

ASSEMBLY

Use whipstitch (see page 16) to attach the pieces on Oakley. Use the long tail to attach each piece.

Attach tummy to center front of body. Attach eyes slightly overlapping top of tummy. Attach pupils to center of eyes.

Stuff beak, and attach between and below eyes.

Flatten wings and attach one to each side of body.

Fold each ear in half and attach (along flat side) to body with cupped opening facing forward.

Weave in ends.

Babies crave time on their tummies—it's a chance to strengthen their neck muscles and begin that all-important wiggling that develops into crawling. But no one wants to be bored on their tummy. So, I designed this colorful play mat, featuring crinkle tabs that give baby something fun to play with! This mat is backed with a piece of felt for stability.

SKILL LEVEL: Beginner

SIZE: 29" x 49", blocked

GAUGE

16 sts x 20 rows in sc = 4" square

MATERIALS

Yarns

220 Superwash from Cascade (100% superwash wool; 3.5 oz; 220 yds) (4)

   A 2 skeins in color 1961 Camel

   B 2 skeins in color 1973 Seafoam Heather

   C 2 skeins in color 836 Pink Ice

   D 2 skeins in color 851 Lime

   E 1 skein in color 842 Light Iris

Hooks and Notions

Size H-8 (5 mm) crochet hook

Sewing thread and sewing needle

Crocheter's toolbox supplies (see page 8)

4" x 8" crinkle paper

1½ yards of felt, ¼" thick, 36" wide (see "Felt" on page 7)

SQUARES

Make 8: 2 *each* in A, B, and C; 1 each in D and E.

With selected color, ch 49.

Row 1: Turn, sc in 2nd ch from hook and each st across. 48 sts

Rows 2–59: Ch 1, turn, sc in each st across.

Fasten off with long tail.

TABS

Make 3.

With D, ch 24.

Rnd 1: Sc in first st (to join in circle), and each st across. 24 sts

Rnds 2–8: Sc in each st.

Fasten off with long tail.

ASSEMBLY

Block (see page 77) squares to 12½" square, so that they're all the same size and have straight edges. Consistency of size among squares is more important than matching measurements.

Assemble squares referring to photo on page 48 as follows: Whipstitch (see page 16) together along horizontal seams and use mattress stitch along vertical seams. Notice each pair of squares is displaced 4" from adjacent pair.

Cut crinkle paper to size of tab and insert 1 piece into each tab. Flatten tab and use long tail to whipstitch closed along final rnd.

With length of D (or your long tail, if you have some left), attach tab to mat at each horizontal seam, slightly offset from vertical seams, as shown in photo.

With sewing thread and running stitch, attach felt to back of mat. Knot and cut thread. Trim felt to shape of mat.

Crinkly Triangle Toy

Crinkle paper and ribbon tabs make this toy absolutely irresistible to anyone small! The most fun part about this project is the chance to browse the world of available ribbons, and select a few that perfectly suit your color scheme. I think you'll find that you can't make just one!

SKILL LEVEL: Beginner

SIZE: 9¼" per side, blocked

GAUGE

8 rnds of sc bl = 4"-diameter circle

MATERIALS

Yardage and materials given for 1 toy.

Yarns

90 yards of Sweater from Spud and Chloe (superwash 55% wool, 45% organic cotton; 3.5 oz; 160 yds) in color 7510 Splash (4)

Alternate colorway in 7508 Pollen

Hooks and Notions

Size H-8 (5 mm) crochet hook

Crocheter's toolbox supplies (see page 8)

Sewing thread, sewing needle, and pins

Five 16" lengths of ribbon, various colors

8" square of crinkle paper

PATTERN NOTE

Work through back loops only.

TRIANGLE

Make 2.

With MC, ch 2.

Rnd 1: Sc 6 times in 2nd ch from hook. 6 sts

Rnd 2: (Sc 3 times in next st, sc in next st) 3 times. 12 sts

Rnd 3: Sc in next st, (sc 3 times in next st, sc in next 3 sts) 2 times, sc 3 times in next st, sc in next 2 sts. 18 sts

Rnd 4: Sc in next 2 sts, (sc 3 times in next st, sc in next 5 sts) 2 times, sc 3 times in next st, sc in next 3 sts. 24 sts

Rnd 5: Sc in next 3 sts, (sc 3 times in next st, sc in next 7 sts) 2 times, sc 3 times in next st, sc in next 4 sts. 30 sts

Cont working rnds in patt as established, working 3 sc in center st of each corner and 2 more sc on each side of triangle until each side has 29 sts, for 16 rnds. 96 sts total

Fasten off with long tail.

ASSEMBLY

Block pieces (see page 77) to schematic measurements below.

Cut 4" lengths of each color of ribbon. Fold each ribbon in half, WS tog, and pin along WS of 1 triangle. Position so that 4 ribbons are evenly spaced along each side of triangle and 1 at each corner.

Cut crinkle paper ½" smaller than triangle.

Position WS of second triangle directly on top of first triangle with crinkle paper inside. Stitch together using running stitch (see page 15) and sewing thread along center of last row of sts. Knot and cut off thread. With new piece of sewing thread, stitch through all layers at rnd 1 to tack layers tog in center. Knot and cut off thread.

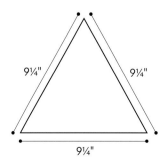

Babies love a rattle. Inspired by bubbles, I designed this rattle to look like a bubble wand: a circle with oodles of bubbles pouring out. The bubbles contain a rattle insert, so there's no doubt baby will adore this toy, regardless of whether he grasps the whole bubble-inspiration thing.

SKILL LEVEL: Beginner

SIZE: Approx 6", including bubbles, stuffed

GAUGE

9 rnds in sc = 3¾"-diameter circle

MATERIALS

Yardage and materials given for 1 rattle.

Yarns

Vickie Howell Sheep(ish) from Bernat (70% acrylic, 30% wool; 3 oz; 167 yds) (4)

  MC 50 yards in color 10 Camel(ish)

  CC 30 yards in color 8 Pink(ish)

Alternate colorway in 10 Camel(ish) and 18 Robin Egg(ish)

Hooks and Notions

Size H-8 (5 mm) crochet hook

Crocheter's toolbox supplies (see page 8)

Two 1" rattle inserts

Polyester stuffing

RING

With MC, ch 24.

Rnd 1: Sc in first st, forming ring, sc in each st around. 24 sts

Rnd 2: Sc in each st.

Rnd 3: (Sc twice in next st, sc in next 3 sts) 6 times. 30 sts

Rnd 4: (Sc twice in next st, sc in next 4 sts) 6 times. 36 sts

Rnd 5: (Sc twice in next st, sc in next 5 sts) 6 times. 42 sts

Rnd 6: (Sc twice in next st, sc in next 6 sts) 6 times. 48 sts

Rnd 7: (Sc twice in next st, sc in next 7 sts) 6 times. 54 sts

Rnds 8–12: Sc in each st.

Rnd 13: (Sc2tog, sc in next 7 sts) 6 times. 48 sts

Rnd 14: (Sc2tog, sc in next 6 sts) 6 times. 42 sts

Rnd 15: (Sc2tog, sc in next 5 sts) 6 times. 36 sts

Rnd 16: (Sc2tog, sc in next 4 sts) 6 times. 30 sts

Rnd 17: (Sc2tog, sc in next 3 sts) 6 times. 24 sts

Fasten off with long tail.

BUBBLE

Make 5.

With CC, ch 2.

Rnd 1: Sc 6 times in 2nd ch from hook. 6 sts

Rnd 2: Sc twice in each st. 12 sts

Rnd 3: (Sc twice in next st, sc in next st) 6 times. 18 sts

Rnds 4–6: Sc in each st.

Rnd 7: (Sc2tog, sc in next st) 6 times. 12 sts

Fasten off with long tail.

ASSEMBLY AND FINISHING

Fold ring so that last rnd and foundation ch meet. With long tail, whipstitch (see page 16) these 2 edges tog, adding stuffing as you go. It should look like a donut.

Stuff each bubble, adding a mini rattle to 2 bubbles. Place 6 markers, evenly spaced around perimeter of ring, and attach bubbles to rnds 8–11 of ring at 5 of the markers. Leaving 6th spot open gives baby a convenient place to hold!

Weave in ends.

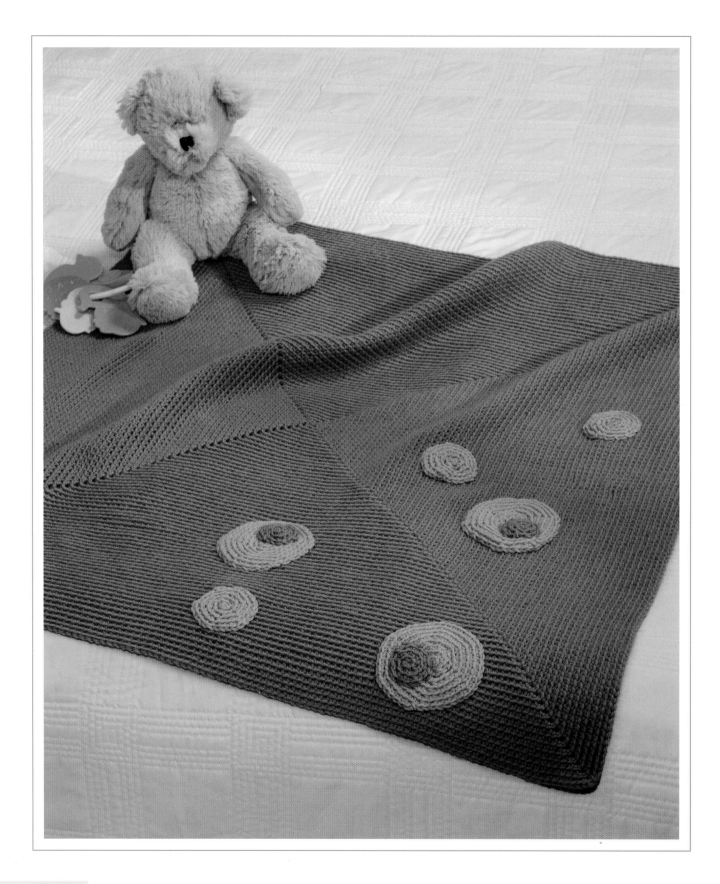

Asymmetrical Circles Blanket

Children of all ages love bubbles. Bubbles reflect the light and always look like they have a bit of asymmetry to them. I designed this blanket to reflect those dancing bubbles. The asymmetrical appliqués are an interesting modern touch, accomplished by creative positioning of circle shapes.

SKILL LEVEL: Easy

SIZE: 33" square, blocked

GAUGE

Large circle = 3½" diameter

MATERIALS

Yardage and materials given for 1 blanket.

Yarns

220 Superwash from Cascade (100% superwash wool; 3.5 oz; 220 yds) **(4)**

MC 5 skeins in color 1961 Camel

CC 1 skein in color 1973 Seafoam Heather

Hooks and Notions

Size H-8 (5 mm) crochet hook

Crocheter's toolbox supplies (see page 8)

PATTERN NOTE

Work through back loops only.

BLANKET

With MC, ch 2.

Rnd 1: Sc 4 times in 2nd ch from hook. 4 sts

Rnd 2: Sc twice in each st. 8 sts

Rnd 3: (Sc 3 times in st, sc in next st) 4 times. 16 sts

Rnd 4: Sc in next st, (sc 3 times in next st, sc in next 3 sts) 3 times, sc 3 times in next st, sc in next 2 sts. 24 sts

Rnd 5: Sc in next 2 sts, (sc 3 times in next st, sc in next 5 sts) 3 times, sc 3 times in next st, sc in next 3 sts. 32 sts

Rnd 6: Sc in next 3 sts, (sc 3 times in next st, sc in next 7 sts) 3 times, sc 3 times in next st, sc in next 4 sts. 40 sts

Cont working rnds in patt as established, working 3 sc in center st of each corner and 2 more sc on each side of square until blanket measures approx 31" square (133 sts per side). 532 sts total

Final rnd: Cont patt to final corner, do not work last side. Fasten off.

Quick Tip for Corners

After a couple of rounds, you'll notice that there is a hole in each of the four corners of the blanket, which is created every time you single crochet three times in the same stitch. All you need to remember to keep your square pattern is to single crochet three times into the center stitch when you see this hole. The rest of the time, you just single crochet around and around!

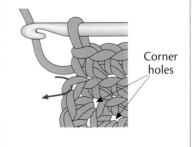

Corner holes

CIRCLE

Make 3 medium in CC, 3 large in CC, and 3 small in MC (9 total).

All Sizes

With selected color, ch 2.

Rnd 1: Sc 6 times in 2nd ch from hook. 6 sts

Rnd 2: Sc twice in each st. 12 sts

Rnd 3: (Sc twice in next st, sc in next st) 6 times. 18 sts

For small, fasten off with long tail.

Medium and Large

Rnd 4: (Sc twice in next st, sc in next 2 sts) 6 times. 24 sts

Rnd 5: (Sc twice in next st, sc in next 3 sts) 6 times. 30 sts

For medium, fasten off with long tail.

Large Only

Rnd 6: (Sc twice in next st, sc in next 4 sts) 6 times. 36 sts

Rnd 7: (Sc twice in next st, sc in next 5 sts) 6 times. 42 sts

Rnd 8: (Sc twice in next st, sc in next 6 sts) 6 times. 48 sts

Fasten off with long tail.

ASSEMBLY

Block pieces (see page 77) to schematic measurements below. Use running stitch (see page 15) to attach appliqués.

Using long tail of each CC circle, attach to blanket. The circles should have a random look about them, concentrated roughly in one quadrant of the blanket. Attach small MC circles to large circles so that they are off-center. If circles appear puffy, place a running stitch around rnd 2 of CC circles to tack them down.

Weave in ends.

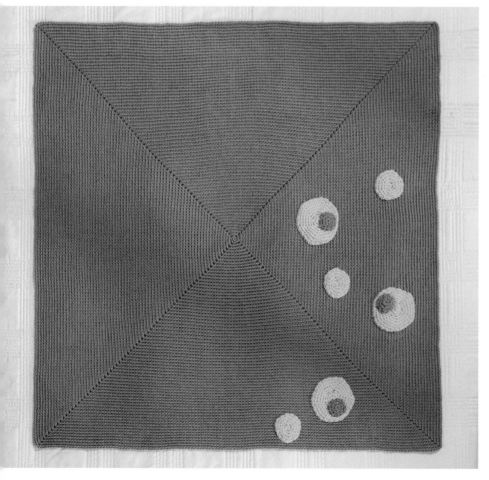

Alternate colorway in 1961 Camel and 836 Pink Ice

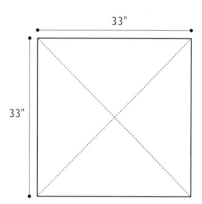

ASYMMETRICAL CIRCLES BLANKET

NATURALLY NEUTRAL

Waves of White Afghan

I'm a sucker for heirloom blankets. Inspired by a simple ruffle pattern, I designed this blanket to look classic, but with a modern twist. The result reminds me of the waves of an ocean, making this the perfect piece for cuddling as you lull your little one to sleep.

SKILL LEVEL: Easy

SIZE: 36" x 37½", before blocking

GAUGE

11 sts x 7 rows of dc = 3¾" square

MATERIALS

Yarn

10 skeins of Worsted Cotton from Blue Sky Alpacas (100% organic cotton; 3.5 oz; 150 yards) in color 614 Drift (4)

Hooks and Notions

Size I-9 (5.5 mm) crochet hook

Crocheter's toolbox supplies (see page 8)

BLANKET

Ch 102.

Row 1: Dc in 4th ch from hook and each ch (ch 3 counts as 1 dc). 100 dc

Rows 2–6: Ch 3, turn, dc in each st across.

Row 7: Ch 3, turn, dc 3 times in each st across until 1 st rem, dc in final st. 296 sts

Row 8: Ch 3, turn, dc in each st across.

Row 9: Ch 3, turn, dc3tog in each st across until 1 st rem, dc in final st. 100 sts

Rows 10–18: Ch 3, turn, dc in each st across.

Work rows 7–18 another 3 times.

Rep rows 7–15 once.

Do not fasten off.

BORDER

To work border, cont from your last st, working your way around the blanket.

Rnd 1: Ch 1, *sc twice in each st along side, sc in each st along next edge; rep from * once, sl st in ch at start of rnd. 448 sts

Rnd 2: Ch 3, dc twice in each st, sl st in top of ch-3 at start of rnd. 896 sts

Rnd 3: Ch 3, dc in each st around, sl st in top of ch-3 at start of rnd. 896 sts

Fasten off.

FINISHING

Weave in ends. Block (see page 77) and gently position the ruffles as you lay blanket flat to dry. With this blanket, it is possible to stretch the dc rows open so it will have a lacy look, but I find that this distorts the overall shape.

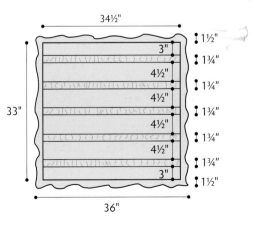

It's easy to be dazzled by the simplicity and beauty of a sea urchin. I designed this pouf to mimic that beauty by working evenly spaced bobbles to create a graceful overall design. This pouf can be happily used by Mom as an ottoman, or as a support that the little one can use when beginning to pull up. Chunky yarn, a big hook, and mostly single crochet means this statement piece will work up quickly!

SKILL LEVEL: Intermediate

SIZE: Approx 21" x 11", stuffed

GAUGE

4 rnds of sc bl = 4¼"-diameter circle

MATERIALS

Yarn

5 skeins of Magnum from Cascade (100% Peruvian highland wool; 8.82 oz; 123 yds), in color 0010 Ecru **⑥**

Hooks and Notions

Size N/P-15 (10 mm) crochet hook

Crocheter's toolbox supplies (see page 8)

21" ottoman base (see "A Perfect Pouf" on page 62)

PATTERN NOTES

Crochet through back loops only, except when completing bobble stitch (see page 13).

POUF COVER

Ch 2.

Rnd 1: Sc 6 times in 2nd ch from hook. 6 sts

Rnd 2: Sc twice in each st. 12 sts.

Rnd 3: (Bbl in next st, sc in bl of *same* st, sc in next st) 6 times. 18 sts

Rnd 4: (Sc twice in next st, sc in next 2 sts) 6 times. 24 sts

Rnd 5: (Bbl in next st, sc in bl of *same* st, sc in next 3 sts) 6 times. 30 sts

Rnd 6: (Sc twice in next st, sc in next 4 sts) 6 times. 36 sts

Rnd 7: (Bbl in next st, sc in bl of *same* st, sc in next 5 sts) 6 times. 42 sts

Rnd 8: (Sc twice in next st, sc in next 6 sts) 6 times. 48 sts

Rnd 9: (Bbl in next st, sc in bl of *same* st, sc in next 7 sts) 6 times. 54 sts

Rnd 10: (Sc twice in next st, sc in next 8 sts) 6 times. 60 sts

Rnds 11–21: Cont working rnds in patt as established, working a rnd of 6 evenly spaced inc with bbl, followed by sc-only rnd of 6 evenly spaced inc, for 11 rnds (last rnd worked has bbls). 126 sts

Rnd 22: Sc in each st around.

Rnd 23: Bbl, sc in next 20 sts.

Rnds 24–33: Rep rnds 22 and 23.

Insert ottoman base or 2 pillow forms into pouf (see "A Perfect Pouf" on page 62). Cont to crochet, enclosing form.

Rnd 34: (Sc2tog, sc in next 19 sts) 6 times. 120 sts

Rnd 35: (Sc2tog, sc in next 18 sts) 6 times. 114 sts

Rnd 36: (Sc2tog, sc in next 17 sts) 6 times. 108 sts

Rnd 37: (Sc2tog, sc in next 16 sts) 6 times. 102 sts

Rnd 38: (Sc2tog, sc in next 15 sts) 6 times. 96 sts

Cont working rnds in patt as established, working 6 evenly spaced dec every rnd until 12 sts rem, for 14 rnds.

Fasten off, leaving 6" tail.

FINISHING

Using tapestry needle, run tail through rem sts, pulling closed. Knot and pull tail to inside.

A Perfect Pouf

I *knew* the nursery needed a pouf, but finding the proper-sized pillow form proved quite difficult. Here's my easy solution: I took two 24"-square pillow forms, stacked them atop one another, and wrapped a length of scrap white yarn around them until they formed a lovely round shape. Easy! And no fancy materials required!

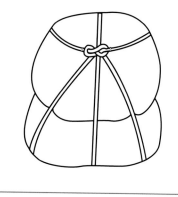

Teddy Bear Bookends

We know that even the littlest ones benefit from the soothing sound they hear when you read a story. I was inspired by my own beloved childhood teddy bear to design a set of bookends. Pellets inside each bear add weight and make them practical for holding books. But keep reading for tips on how to convert them to cuddly playthings!

SKILL LEVEL: Easy

SIZE: Approx 8" tall, stuffed

GAUGE

Body at end of rnd 7 = 4"-diameter circle

MATERIALS

Yardage and materials given for pair of bookends.

Yarns

Nature's Choice Organic Cotton from Lion Brand (100% organically grown cotton; 3 oz; 103 yds) (4)

> MC 2 skeins in color 480-098 Almond*
>
> CC 2 skeins in color 480-099 Macadamia*

Hooks and Notions

Size H-8 (5 mm) crochet hook

Crocheter's toolbox supplies (see page 8)

Polyester stuffing

1 lb of Poly-Pellets

2 nylon knee-high stockings

Four 12 mm colored animal eyes

*To make second bear, reverse colors.

PATTERN NOTES

Work through back loops only.

Instructions make one bear. Repeat instructions, reversing colors, to make second bear.

BODY

With MC, ch 2.

Rnd 1: Sc 6 times in 2nd ch from hook. 6 sts

Rnd 2: Sc twice in each st. 12 sts

Rnd 3: (Sc twice in next st, sc in next st) 6 times. 18 sts

Rnd 4: (Sc twice in next st, sc in next 2 sts) 6 times. 24 sts

Rnd 5: (Sc twice in next st, sc in next 3 sts) 6 times. 30 sts

Rnd 6: (Sc twice in next st, sc in next 4 sts) 6 times. 36 sts

Rnd 7: (Sc twice in next st, sc in next 5 sts) 6 times. 42 sts

Rnd 8: (Sc twice in next st, sc in next 6 sts) 6 times. 48 sts

Rnds 9–13: Sc in each st.

Rnd 14: (Sc2tog, sc in next 6 sts) 6 times. 42 sts

Rnds 15 and 16: Sc in each st.

Rnd 17: (Sc2tog, sc in next 5 sts) 6 times. 36 sts

Rnds 18 and 19: Sc in each st.

Rnd 20: (Sc2tog, sc in next 4 sts) 6 times. 30 sts

Rnds 21 and 22: Sc in each st.

Fasten off.

HEAD

Work as for body to end of rnd 7. 42 sts

Rnds 8–13: Sc in each st.

Rnd 14: (Sc2tog, sc in next 5 sts) 6 times. 36 sts

Rnd 15: (Sc2tog, sc in next 4 sts) 6 times. 30 sts

Fasten off with long tail.

●●●○ TEDDY BEAR BOOKENDS

ARM

Make 2.

With MC, ch 2.

Rnd 1: Sc 6 times in 2nd ch from hook. 6 sts

Rnd 2: Sc twice in each st. 12 sts

Rnd 3: (Sc twice in next st, sc in next st) 6 times. 18 sts

Rnds 4–6: Sc in each st.

Rnd 7: (Sc2tog, sc in next st) 6 times. 12 sts

Rnds 8–12: Sc in each st.

Fasten off with long tail.

FOOT

Make 2.

With CC, ch 2.

Rnd 1: Sc 6 times in 2nd ch from hook. 6 sts

Rnd 2: Sc twice in each st. 12 sts

Rnd 3: (Sc twice in next st, sc in next st) 6 times. 18 sts

Rnd 4: (Sc twice in next st, sc in next 2 sts) 6 times. 24 sts

Rnds 5 and 6: With body color, sc in each st.

Rnd 7: (Sc2tog, sc in next 2 sts) 6 times. 18 sts

Rnd 8: (Sc2tog, sc in next st) 6 times. 12 sts

Fasten off with long tail.

SNOUT

With CC, ch 2.

Rnd 1: Sc 6 times in 2nd ch from hook. 6 sts

Rnd 2: Sc twice in each st. 12 sts

Rnd 3: (Sc twice in next st, sc in next st) 6 times. 18 sts

Rnd 4: (Sc twice in next st, sc in next 2 sts) 6 times. 24 sts

Rnd 5: Sc in each st.

Fasten off with long tail.

NOSE

With MC, ch 2.

Sc 6 times in 2nd ch from hook. 6 sts

Fasten off with long tail.

EAR

Make 2.

With MC, ch 2.

Rnd 1: Sc 6 times in 2nd ch from hook. 6 sts.

Rnd 2: Sc twice in each st. 12 sts.

Rnd 3: (Sc twice in next st, sc in next st) 6 times. 18 sts.

Rnds 4 and 5: Sc in each st.

Fasten off with long tail.

ASSEMBLY

For assembly of all pieces, use long tail of each piece and whipstitch (see page 16) to attach.

Attach nose to rnds 3 and 4 of snout. Stuff snout and attach to rnds 7–12 of head. Flatten ears and attach to sides of head, vertically, from rnds 5–10. Fasten eyes between rnds 7 and 8 of head.

Stuff feet and attach to rnds 8–12 of body, positioning them close together so they sit at front of body. Stuff arms, flatten, and attach to rnd 20 at each side of body.

Fill nylon stocking with Poly-Pellets until fist-sized (approx ½ lb of pellets). Stocking prevents pellets from leaking out between crochet stitches. Tie off stocking. Fill remaining body with stuffing. Stuff head.

Attach head and body, pulling whipstitches gently every few stitches in order to create neck.

Make a Cuddly Teddy!

These bears are designed to be bookends, and the polyester pellets and plastic eyes aren't for babies to play with. But, with two simple steps, you can easily adapt the pattern into an adorable stuffed animal that's safe for babies.

For a toy, do not use the pellets. Instead, fill the entire body with stuffing.

For baby-safe eyes, crochet two eyes following the instructions on page 8 and using your desired color of yarn. Attach the eyes as you would any other piece.

Presto! Cuddly teddy!

I adore the combination of white, gray, and black. In some settings, these colors can appear cold, but used together in a squishy rug, they make perfect sense. The increases in this design create an interesting swirling pattern. It's a happy accident that's incredibly easy to crochet, but looks complicated and sophisticated in the end.

SKILL LEVEL: Easy

SIZE: 26" diameter, blocked

GAUGE

Rug at end of rnd 9 = 3¾"-diameter circle

MATERIALS

Yarns

Cotton-Ease from Lion Brand (50% cotton, 50% acrylic; 3.5 oz; 207 yds) 【4】

A 1 skein in color 830-100 Snow

B 1 skein in color 830-149 Stone

C 1 skein in color 830-152 Charcoal

Hooks and Notions

Size H-8 (5 mm) crochet hook

Sewing thread and sewing needle

Crocheter's toolbox supplies (see page 8)

1 yard of felt, ¼"-thick, 36" wide (see "Felt" on page 7)

Nonskid backing (optional)

PATTERN NOTE

Let unused yarn float along back of work.

RUG

With A, ch 2.

Rnd 1: Sc 6 times in 2nd ch from hook. 6 sts

Rnd 2: Ch 1, sc twice in each st, sl st in ch at beg of rnd. 12 sts

Rnd 3: With B, ch 1, (sc twice in next st, sc in next st) 6 times, sl st in ch at beg of rnd. 18 sts

Rnd 4: Ch 1, (sc twice in next st, sc in next 2 sts) 6 times, sl st in ch at beg of rnd. 24 sts

Rnd 5: With C, ch 1, (sc twice in next st, sc in next 3 sts) 6 times, sl st in ch at beg of rnd. 30 sts

Rnd 6: Ch 1, (sc twice in next st, sc in next 4 sts) 6 times, sl st in ch at beg of rnd. 36 sts

Rnd 7: With A, ch 1, (sc twice in next st, sc in next 5 sts) 6 times, sl st in ch at beg of rnd. 42 sts

Rnd 8: Ch 1, (sc twice in next st, sc in next 6 sts) 6 times, sl st in ch at beg of rnd. 48 sts

Cont working rnds in patt as established, changing color every 2 rnds (B, C, then A) and working 6 evenly spaced inc every rnd until piece measures 26" across. 372 sts total

Fasten off.

FINISHING

Weave in ends. Block your piece (see page 77) to schematic measurements below so that it lies smooth and flat.

Pin together your rug, felt, and nonskid backing (if using it). With sewing thread and running stitch (see page 15), sew along the final round, and then around a few inner rounds to tack in place. Knot and cut off thread.

Trim felt and backing to same size as rug.

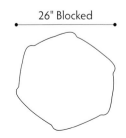

26" Blocked

Buzzy Bee Mobile

Bees are nature's wonder, industrious, never-tiring makers of honey. I have a carpenter bee that lives in a piece of wood on my patio. While I'm crocheting, he buzzes around me, always focused on his job, and always making a lovely buzzing sound. These bees don't buzz, but I hope they'll remind you of the wondrous qualities of these tiny workers.

SKILL LEVEL: Easy

SIZE: Hive 6" tall, stuffed; mobile width and height determined by tree branch and bee positions

GAUGE

9 rnds of sc = 3¾"-diameter circle

MATERIALS

Yarns

Vickie Howell Sheep(ish) from Bernat (70% acrylic, 30% wool; 3 oz; 167 yds) (4)

- **MC** 115 yards in color 10 Camel(ish)
- **A** 25 yards in color 12 Yellow(ish)
- **B** 25 yards in color 1 Black(ish)

Hooks and Notions

Size H-8 (5 mm) crochet hook

Crocheter's toolbox supplies (see page 8)

Polyester stuffing

Approx 14"-long tree branch (check that your branch isn't too heavy for your thread)

Nylon monofilament thread (or fishing line, 8 lb test)

8 beading crimps

Crimping pliers

1"-diameter metal key ring

Try Ribbon, Instead!

Want to skip the hassle of monofilament and crimps?

Use ⅛"-wide ribbon, instead. Your bees won't look like they're flying in midair, but the assembly process will be much easier!

HIVE SEGMENTS

Make 1 of each size; instructions are for small (medium, large, jumbo). Where one number or set of instructions appears, it applies to all sizes.

With MC, ch 2.

Rnd 1: Sc 6 times in 2nd ch from hook. 6 sts

Rnd 2: Sc twice in each st. 12 sts

Rnd 3: (Sc twice in next st, sc in next st) 6 times. 18 sts

Rnd 4: (Sc twice in next st, sc in next 2 sts) 6 times. 24 sts

Rnd 5: (Sc twice in next st, sc in next 3 sts) 6 times. 30 sts

Small

Rnds 6–8: Sc in each st. 30 sts

Skip to rnd 21 on page 70.

All Other Sizes

Rnd 6: (Sc twice in next st, sc in next 4 sts) 6 times. 36 sts

Rnd 7: (Sc twice in next st, sc in next 5 sts) 6 times. 42 sts

Medium

Rnds 8–10: Sc in each st. 42 sts

Skip to rnd 19 below.

All Other Sizes

Rnd 8: (Sc twice in next st, sc in next 6 sts) 6 times. 48 sts

Rnd 9: (Sc twice in next st, sc in next 7 sts) 6 times. 54 sts

Large

Rnds 10–12: Sc in each st. 54 sts

Skip to rnd 17 below.

Jumbo

Rnd 10: (Sc twice in next st, sc in next 8 sts) 6 times. 60 sts

Rnd 11: (Sc twice in next st, sc in next 9 sts) 6 times. 66 sts

Rnds 12–14: Sc in each st. 66 sts

Rnd 15: (Sc2tog, sc in next 9 sts) 6 times. 60 sts

Rnd 16: (Sc2tog, sc in next 8 sts) 6 times. 54 sts

Rnd 17: (Sc2tog, sc in next 7 sts) 6 times. 48 sts

Rnd 18: (Sc2tog, sc in next 6 sts) 6 times. 42 sts

Rnd 19: (Sc2tog, sc in next 5 sts) 6 times. 36 sts

Rnd 20: (Sc2tog, sc in next 4 sts) 6 times. 30 sts

Rnd 21: (Sc2tog, sc in next 3 sts) 6 times. 24 sts

Stuff hive segment and cont as follows:

Rnd 22: (Sc2tog, sc in next 2 sts) 6 times. 18 sts

Rnd 23: (Sc2tog, sc in next st) 6 times. 12 sts

Rnd 24: (Sc2tog) 6 times. 6 sts

Rnd 25: Sc next and 4th st tog, rem sts unworked. 1 st

Fasten off, pulling tail to inside.

BEE

Make 5.

With A, ch 2.

Rnd 1: Sc 6 times in 2nd ch from hook. 6 sts

Rnd 2: Sc twice in each st. 12 sts

Rnd 3: (Sc twice in next st, sc in next st) 6 times. 18 sts

Rnd 4: Sc in each st.

Rnds 5–9: Rep rnd 4, working 2 rnds in B, then 2 rnds in A, then 1 rnd in B.

Rnd 10: (Sc2tog, sc in next st) 6 times. 12 sts

Stuff your bee and cont as follows:

Rnd 11: (Sc2tog) 6 times. 6 sts

Rnd 12: Sc next and 4th st tog, rem sts unworked. 1 st

Fasten off, pulling tail to inside.

ASSEMBLY

Stack hive segments in order of descending size. Thread tapestry needle with length of MC, and pass needle through center of each piece. Return needle through to starting point, and pull yarn taut. Knot, pulling tail to inside.

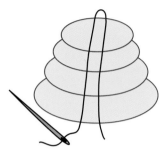

To assemble mobile, attach length of monofilament to each bee and tie to tree branch. Attach a length of monofilament to hive and tie to center of branch. I use a beading crimp above each knot. Monofilament can be slippery, and you don't want your knot to come undone!

Tie three lengths of monofilament through the key ring and then wrap the thread around the branch for hanging. The exact position of each hanging thread will depend on the balance of your particular branch.

I love the look of a classic basket-weave afghan, but I just felt like it was a little too symmetrical. A modern nursery is all about bringing in an unexpected detail. The pale gray isn't a color typically associated with babies, but when combined with a lovely pattern, I think it's a blanket that fits perfectly wrapped around your little one.

SKILL LEVEL: Intermediate

SIZE: 32" square, blocked

GAUGE

12 sts x 7 rows of dc = 3½" square

MATERIALS

Yarn

9 skeins of Martha Stewart Crafts Extra Soft Wool Blend (65% acrylic, 35% wool; 3.5 oz; 165 yds) in color 5400-550 Gray Pearl (4)

Hooks and Notions

Size I-9 (5.5 mm) crochet hook

Crocheter's toolbox supplies (see page 8)

PATTERN NOTE

This pattern makes use of back-post double crochet and front-post double crochet (see page 12).

BLANKET

Ch 104.

Row 1 (WS): Turn, dc in 4th ch from hook and each st across (ch 3 counts as dc). 102 sts

Rows 2–21: Ch 2 (ch 2 counts as dc), turn, bpdc in 25 sts, fpdc in 25 sts, bpdc in 25 sts, fpdc in 25 sts, dc in last st. 102 dc

Row 22 (RS): Ch 2, turn, bpdc in 25 sts, fpdc in 25 sts, bpdc in 50 sts, dc in last st.

Row 23 (WS): Ch 2, turn, fpdc in 50 sts, bpdc in 25 sts, fpdc in 25 sts, dc in last st.

Rows 24–43: Work rows 22 and 23 for 10 times.

Row 44: Ch 2, turn, bpdc in 25 sts, fpdc in 75 sts, dc in last st.

Row 45: Ch 2, turn, bpdc in 75 sts, fpdc in 25 sts, dc in last st.

Rows 46–65: Work rows 44 and 45 for 10 times.

Row 66: Ch 2, turn, bpdc in 100 sts, dc in last st.

Row 67: Ch 2, turn, fpdc in 100 sts, dc in last st.

Rows 68–87: Work rows 66 and 67 for 10 times.

Row 88: Rep row 66.

Do not fasten off.

BORDER

To work border, cont from your last st, working around blanket.

Rotate blanket 90° clockwise, and sc 100 sts along the side. (Helpful tip: This means that you will sc in each edge dc and tch and sc twice approx every 5 sts.) Sc 100 sts along foundation ch, sc 100 sts along 2nd side (using same method as for first side), sc 100 sts along final row. Use locking stitch markers to mark corner sts.

Border rnd: Crocheting through bl, sc 3 times in each corner st, and once in each st around.

Cont working border rows until border measures 2", for approx 7 rnds.

Fasten off.

FINISHING

Weave in ends. Block blanket (see page 77) to schematic measurements so that it lies nice and flat!

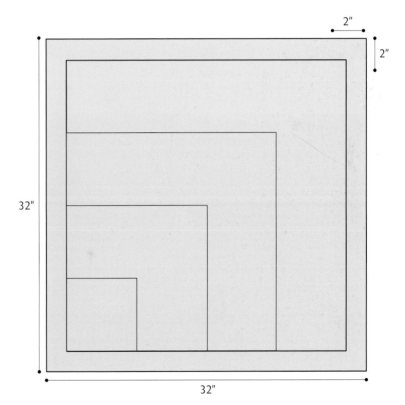

Birds are the world's morning lovers, always chipper and delighted at the start of each new day. Regardless of whether *you* happen to be so cheery in the morning, a birdy will bring a smile to your face.

SKILL Level: Easy

SIZE: Approx 7" tall, stuffed

GAUGE

Head at end of rnd 8 = 4"-diameter circle

MATERIALS

Yardage and materials given for 1 bird.

Yarns

Martha Stewart Crafts Extra Soft Wool Blend (65% acrylic, 35% wool; 3.5 oz; 165 yds) **(4)**

> **MC** 70 yards in color 5400-500 Bakery Box White

> **CC** 5 yards in color 5400-557 Lemon Chiffon

Alternate colorways in 5400-551 Cobweb and 5400-550 Gray Pearl

Hooks and Notions

Size H-8 (5 mm) crochet hook

Crocheter's toolbox supplies (see page 8)

Polyester stuffing

Two 10 mm black oval plastic animal eyes (optional, see "Baby-Safe Crocheted Eyes" on page 8)

1" squeaker (optional)

PATTERN NOTE

Work through back loops only.

HEAD

With MC, ch 2.

Rnd 1: Sc 6 times in 2nd ch from hook. 6 sts

Rnd 2: Sc twice in each st. 12 sts

Rnd 3: (Sc twice in next st, sc in next st) 6 times. 18 sts

Rnd 4: (Sc twice in next st, sc in next 2 sts) 6 times. 24 sts

Rnd 5: (Sc twice in next st, sc in next 3 sts) 6 times. 30 sts

Rnd 6: (Sc twice in next st, sc in next 4 sts) 6 times. 36 sts

Rnds 7–11: Sc in each st.

Rnd 12: (Sc2tog, sc in next 4 sts) 6 times. 30 sts

Rnd 13: (Sc2tog, sc in next 3 sts) 6 times. 24 sts

Fasten off with long tail.

BODY

With MC, ch 2.

Rnd 1: Sc 6 times in 2nd ch from hook. 6 sts

Rnd 2: Sc twice in each st. 12 sts

Rnd 3: (Sc twice in next st, sc in next st) 6 times. 18 sts

Rnd 4: (Sc twice in next st, sc in next 2 sts) 6 times. 24 sts

Rnd 5: (Sc twice in next st, sc in next 3 sts) 6 times. 30 sts

Rnd 6: (Sc twice in next st, sc in next 4 sts) 6 times. 36 sts

Rnd 7: (Sc twice in next st, sc in next 5 sts) 6 times. 42 sts

Rnd 8: (Sc twice in next st, sc in next 6 sts) 6 times. 48 sts

Rnds 9–16: Sc in each st.

Rnd 17: (Sc2tog, sc in next 6 sts) 6 times. 42 sts

Rnd 18: (Sc2tog, sc in next 5 sts) 6 times. 36 sts

Rnd 19: (Sc2tog, sc in next 4 sts) 6 times. 30 sts

Rnd 20: (Sc2tog, sc in next 3 sts) 6 times. 24 sts

Stuff body and insert squeaker in center of stuffing, if using one.

Rnd 21: (Sc2tog, sc in next 2 sts) 6 times. 18 sts

Rnds 22–33: Sc in each st.

Fasten off with long tail.

BEAK

With CC, ch 2.

Rnd 1: Sc 6 times in 2nd ch from hook. 6 sts

Rnd 2: Sc twice in each st. 12 sts

Rnd 3: Sc in each st. 12 sts

Fasten off with long tail.

ASSEMBLY

Use whipstitch (see page 16) and long tail to attach pieces.

Slightly stuff beak. Attach to head at rnd 4. Fasten eyes to head (or use crocheted versions, see page 8). Stuff head. Attach head to rnds 9–14 of body.

Weave in ends.

Finishing and Care

I know that the fun part is doing the actual crocheting, but keep in mind that finishing your piece is a key part of getting a beautiful finished product!

BLOCKING

The word blocking can put fear into the heart of many crocheters, but it doesn't have to be complicated!

Why Block?

As you crochet, the yarn comes fresh off the skein and gets all worked up into your piece. Over time, the yarn in your stitches will relax, possibly changing the size of your piece. What blocking does is speed up this process, morphing your piece into its finished size.

When making a project that is multiple pieces sewn together (such as the Mondrian-Inspired Afghan on page 19), it's important to block the pieces before you assemble them. Why? Let's imagine that you assemble your pieces immediately after crocheting. Later, when you wash your blanket (you know you will—it's for a baby!), the individual pieces will expand, but the seams won't. This will leave your piece looking sloppy. And there's no way to unwash the blanket to get it to its original shape.

So, take the little bit of extra time to block when it's specified in your pattern. If an item will never be washed (like a mobile), then blocking isn't necessary and you don't have to do it. Which means, if I *do* mention blocking in project instructions, it's because it's important!

How to Block

Blocking involves getting your piece wet and laying it out to dry in the dimensions specified. There are two ways to do it.

In the washing machine. If you're using a machine-washable yarn (see "Machine-Washable Yarns" on page 5), then you can toss your piece(s) in the machine and wash, following the washing instructions on the yarn label. The advantage to this method is that the spinning of the washing machine will leave your piece with very little water remaining.

If your pieces have long tails (which will later be used for assembling), then you will need to take caution to make sure that the long pieces of yarn don't get wrapped around the agitator. Either use a front-loading machine, place your pieces in a garment bag, or hand wash them (see below). Remove the work from the machine and let dry (see below).

By hand. If you're using a yarn that's not machine washable or you just feel like the hands-on approach, it's easy to block by hand. Fill a sink or tub with water (and optional wool wash) and let the piece soak for about 15 minutes. Then gently squeeze as much water out as you can and let dry.

Let dry. For both methods, the drying technique is the same: Lay out a towel (or two) and put your piece on top. Smooth the piece with your hands, shifting the edges so that the piece is the desired shape and size. Many larger pieces will dry in the shape you give them but, if you notice the edges curling, don't hesitate to pin the edges down. When it's dry, you're done!

WASHING

Let's be honest: these pieces are made for babies, meaning that they'll need to be cleaned.

For blankets, you'll wash them the same way you would for blocking a piece. Use an appropriate detergent for your method (machine or hand), and follow the instructions for blocking above.

For pieces that are stuffed (such as toys and pillows), machine washing is acceptable, but numerous washings may cause the stuffing to shift or clump over time. For the longest life of your piece, it's best to spot clean small oopsies.

Useful Information

Yarn-Weight Symbol and Category Name	(1) Super Fine	(2) Fine	(3) Light	(4) Medium	(5) Bulky	(6) Super Bulky
Types of Yarn in Category	Sock, Fingering, Baby	Sport, Baby	DK, Light Worsted	Worsted, Afghan, Aran	Chunky, Craft, Rug	Bulky, Roving
Crochet Gauge* Range in Single Crochet to 4"	21 to 32 sts	16 to 20 sts	12 to 17 sts	11 to 14 sts	8 to 11 sts	5 to 9 sts
Recommended Hook in US Size Range	B-1 to E-4	E-4 to 7	7 to I-9	I-9 to K-10½	K-10½ to M-13	M-13 and larger
Recommended Hook in Metric Size Range	2.25 to 3.5 mm	3.5 to 4.5 mm	4.5 to 5.5 mm	5.5 to 6.5 mm	6.5 to 9 mm	9 mm and larger

These are guidelines only. The above reflect the most commonly used gauges and needle or hook sizes for specific yarn categories.

SKILL LEVELS

Beginner: Projects for first-time crocheters using basic stitches; minimal shaping.

Easy: Projects with basic stitches, repetitive stitch patterns, simple color changes, and simple shaping and finishing.

Intermediate: Projects using a variety of techniques, such as basic lace patterns or color patterns; midlevel shaping and finishing.

Experienced: Projects with intricate stitch patterns, techniques, and dimension, such as nonrepeating patterns, multicolor techniques, fine threads, small hooks, detailed shaping, and refined finishing.

METRIC CONVERSIONS

meter(s) = yard(s) x 0.9144

yard(s) = meter(s) x 1.0936

gram(s) = oz x 28.35

oz = gram(s) x 0.0352

Abbreviations and Glossary

( ) Work instructions within parentheses as many times as directed.

* Repeat instructions following the single asterisk as directed.

AC accent color

approx approximate(ly)

beg begin(ning)(s)

bet between

bl back loop(s)

bpdc back-post double crochet

bbl(s) bobble stitch(es) variation

A color A

B color B

CC contrasting color, includes number if more than one in the pattern

ch chain(s)

ch- refers to chain or space previously made, such as ch-1 space

ch st chain st(s)

cont continue(ing)(s)

dc double crochet(s)

dc2(3)tog double crochet together number of specified stitches

dec(s) decrease(ing)(s)

fl front loop(s)

fpdc front-post double crochet

inc(s) increase(ing)(s)

lb pound

MC main color

m meter(s)

mm millimeter(s)

oz ounce(s)

patt pattern(s)

rem remain(ing)

rep repeat(s)

rnd(s) round(s)

RS right side

sc single crochet(s)

sc2(3)tog single crochet together specified number of stitches

sk skip(ping)

sl slip

sp space(s)

st(s) stitch(es)

tch turning chain(s)

tog together

WS wrong side(s)

Resources

Please contact the following manufacturers to learn where you can purchase their products.

YARNS

Bernat
www.bernat.com
Vickie Howell Sheep(ish)

Blue Sky Alpacas
www.blueskyalpacas.com
Blue Sky Alpacas Worsted Cotton

Caron
www.caron.com
Simply Soft

Cascade
www.cascadeyarns.com
220 Superwash, Magnum

Lion Brand
www.lionbrand.com
Baby's First, Cotton-Ease, Martha Stewart Crafts Extra Soft Wool Blend, Nature's Choice Organic Cotton

Spud and Chloe
www.spudandchloe.com
Sweater

HOOKS AND NOTIONS

American Felt and Craft
www.americanfeltandcraft.com
crinkle paper, mini rattle inserts, squeakers

Suncatcher Eyes
www.suncatchereyes.net
Plastic animal eyes of all sizes, including handpainted colors

Acknowledgments

Writing a book takes a village, and this book is no exception. First and foremost, I'd like to send a huge thank-you to the folks at Martingale who made this book come to life.

I do what I do because of the encouragement, cheers, and smiles I receive from my crochet buddies: my students in classes, readers of my blog, fans on Facebook, and of course friends in my Ravelry group. They're always there to bounce an idea off of, get excited along with me about a new design, and dazzle me with their creations made from my patterns. I adore you all. . . . Thank you for making the FreshStitches community the best! And a special thanks to Adriana, who stepped in to do some fabulous sample crocheting!

My biggest support is, without fail, my sweetie, Tim. He's my adventure buddy, best friend, and biggest fan. He even learned to crochet this year, which makes him just a little bit more awesome.

And last but not least, a huge thanks goes out to the yarn companies featured in this book. They create soft and lovely yarn that makes crochet worth doing.

About the Author

Stacey Trock is the designer for FreshStitches Amigurumi, an exciting place where her stuffed animal creations live out very happy and fulfilling lives. At FreshStitches, Stacey lives out her dream of helping people all over the world crochet their own cute creations. She is also the author of *Cuddly Crochet* (Martingale, 2010) and *Crocheted Softies* (Martingale, 2011).

Stacey also adores her gig as a crochet instructor, traveling around the country (and world!) to spread the love of crochet to her students. In addition to teaching in person, Stacey teaches online classes at Craftsy. Her passion for spreading crochet-love bubbles over into the crochet tips and techniques she shares on her blog.

Residing in Minneapolis, Minnesota, Stacey enjoys running, baking, traveling, and most of all, knitting and crocheting.

Photo by Gale Zucker.

Catch Stacey on her website and blog: www.freshstitches.com. Follow her on Twitter: @freshstitches.

What's your creative passion?
Find it at **ShopMartingale.com**
books • eBooks • ePatterns • daily blog • free projects
videos • tutorials • inspiration • giveaways

Create with Confidence